# *Wagner's Ring &*
# *the Germanic Tradition*

Collin Cleary

Wagnerphile Books
2021

Copyright © 2021 by Collin Cleary
All rights reserved

Cover images:

Foreground:
Anton Marussig, *Sonnenwende*, postcard, 1889 or after

Background:
August Heinrich, *The Watzmann Seen from the North-East, and Some Sketches of a Mountain*, 1820–22, Metropolitan Museum of Art

Cover design by
Kevin I. Slaughter

Hardcover ISBN: 978-1-64264-100-4
Paperback ISBN: 978-1-64264-101-1
E-book ISBN: 978-1-64264-102-8

## Contents

Introduction ❖ 1

Chapter 1: Origins of the *Ring* ❖ 7

Chapter 2: The Story of *Der Ring des Nibelungen* ❖ 23

Chapter 3: Wagner's Sources ❖ 35

Chapter 4: Wotan & the Faustian West ❖ 49

Chapter 5: *Das Rheingold* ❖ 69

Chapter 6: *Die Walküre* ❖ 76

Chapter 7: *Siegfried* ❖ 79

Chapter 8: *Götterdämmerung* ❖ 88

Chapter 9: *Gelassenheit* ❖ 93

Appendix: Suggestions for Exploring Wagner ❖ 101

Index ❖ 103

About the Author ❖ 112

# Introduction

Richard Wagner is the man principally responsible for keeping the Germanic mythological tradition alive in the modern world. Countless individuals have been exposed to that tradition through Wagner's *Ring des Nibelungen*, and it is safe to say that at any given moment somewhere in the world some portion of the *Ring* is being played or performed. In other words, at any given moment, by means of the *Ring*, the stories of the gods and heroes are being recounted: the story of the building of Valhalla, of Wotan's (Odin's) sacrifice of an eye, of Siegmund's drawing the sword from the tree, of Siegfried's slaying the dragon, of Siegfried and Brünnhilde's ill-fated love, and of the murder of Siegfried—to name just a few of the mythic elements incorporated into the *Ring*. The myths live and continue to move people thanks to Wagner. And they will continue to do so, for Wagner used the myths as the basis for one of the greatest artworks ever created (arguably *the* greatest—for it is, as Wagner himself claimed, the *total* work of art). The *Ring* is immortal.

Given this, one would think that Germanic neo-heathens, and indeed all aficionados of Germanic myth and legend, would all be fanatical Wagnerites—travelling great distances to see the Ring performed, studying the libretti, collecting the countless recordings by this conductor and that. But with a few exceptions, this is not the case. The most obvious reason for this is that these individuals, whatever good intentions they may have, are still products of their time, unaccustomed to the sort of challenges posed by Wagner. Wagner is "classical music," after all, and not nearly as approachable as Mozart or Bach. His music is not "relaxing."¹ It is frequently unnerving and emotionally moving. His operas are dominated, for the most part, by a kind of Germanic earnestness (which is one of the chief reasons, I suspect, that many find them off-putting). There is little humor. Plus, Wagner is not content merely to tell a story. His works are laden with philosophical meaning (their Schopenhauerian pessimism is surely another reason why some avoid them). Finally, it must be mentioned that virtually every Wagner opera is extremely *long*, and even Wagner fanatics find themselves nodding off at times. Wagner is not for people with short attention spans.

Still, there is another major reason why lovers of Germanic mythology resist Wagner, and that has to do with the impression that although Wagner draws on Germanic myth, he also distorts it for his own purposes.² One finds a wide variety of people making this claim. J. R. R. Tolkien, for example, accused Wagner of distorting Northern European myth. An ironic claim given the obvious indebtedness of *The Lord of the Rings*

---

[1] Classical music is currently marketed in the United States as "good for relaxation." As always, everything must be oriented toward commerce and the body. Mozart is "good," therefore, because his music lowers the heart rate and helps one drift off to sleep. One wakes up the next morning refreshed and ready to head back to the office and make more sales. Therefore, Mozart is good because Mozart = money.

[2] Often this is tied to the idea that Wagner was some kind of proto-Nazi—a view typically asserted by people who have no real knowledge of Wagner and only the vaguest idea of what Nazism was. I do not intend to deal with this issue in the present book. However, once I have finished discussing the philosophy behind the *Ring*, intelligent readers will realize how problematic it is to try to link Wagner to National Socialism.

to Wagner (which Tolkien disingenuously denied, saying "Both rings were round, and there the resemblance ceases")—and given Tolkien's insistence on injecting Christian elements into his own mythos (e.g., Frodo as Jesus). Numerous scholars have also taken Wagner to task for "getting the myths wrong." A. T. Hatto is representative here, writing of the *Nibelungenlied*: "Modern poets and poetasters have often returned to its subject, prominent among them Richard Wagner with his gigantic music drama *Der Ring des Nibelungen* with which . . . he has ultimately harmed the cause of medieval German poetry by intruding reckless distortions between us and an ancient masterpiece."[3]

Of course, the obvious response to such an assertion is that Wagner's aim was to produce a work of art, not a piece of scholarship. However, a real defense of Wagner—which is the purpose of this book—will have to be somewhat more elaborate. I intend to argue that Wagner was a remarkably serious student of Germanic myth, and the *Ring* is remarkably faithful to it. I intend to argue, further, that the "changes" he makes to the myths are all legitimate developments of the mythic material. And, most important of all, in developing that material in his own way he was following in the footsteps of the anonymous authors of the *Volsunga saga* and other works, all of whom put their own personal stamp upon their sources. In doing so, they revealed new layers—new *truths*—latent in the sources. The myths and sagas are not fixed and static; in the right hands, they give birth to new ideas and new connections. As we shall see in the case of

---

[3] Quoted in Deryck Cooke, *I Saw the World End: A Sudy of Wagner's Ring* (Oxford: Oxford University Press, 1991), 83.

Wagner, the myths have the power to possess those who take them up.

Furthermore, I will argue for an even stronger and more controversial claim: of all the forms in which the Germanic mythology has been preserved, Wagner's *Der Ring des Nibelungen* is the most beautiful. Wagner is the greatest *skald* who ever lived. There is beauty in the *Eddas* and sagas, but it is a rough beauty mixed with a great deal that is indecorous. There is profundity there too, but it exists alongside a lot that is naïve and unrefined. And as for the *Nibelungenlied*, no honest person has ever felt anything other than disappointment when coming to it after an encounter with Wagner. Indeed, the poetry of Wagner's libretti for the *Ring* is superior to that of the *Nibelungenlied*.

And Wagner's poetry is, in the main, more intellectually profound because Wagner stood on the shoulders of the great German philosophers G. W. F. Hegel, Ludwig Feuerbach, and Arthur Schopenhauer. Indeed, Wagner is the great synthesizer of German myth and German philosophy (the topic of Wagner's place in the Germanic tradition, in fact, covers more than just his appropriation of the myths). Aside from this, of course, Wagner adds still another entirely new dimension to the mythic tradition, and it is really for this above all else that he is celebrated: he sets it to some of the most rapturous music ever written, music which seems to express the very spirit of the tradition itself.

Now, the above claims will scandalize some of my readers. "How can you compare Wagner to the original sources—let alone praise him, in some ways, as superior?" Well, such an objection misses the point and rests on some faulty presuppositions. First of all, virtually every one of the "original sources" dates from Christian times, and many of their authors were

Christian (like Snorri Sturluson) and not "pagan" at all (except, perhaps, in spirit). Second, and most important, one of the major points of this book is to argue that Wagner should be regarded as *one of our sources*. It may very well be that Wagner was more a pagan at heart than Snorri Sturluson. He was certainly a harsh critic of Christianity (and the idea that he came to embrace Christianity in his later period—the period of *Parsifal*—is largely a myth). But the primary reason for regarding Wagner as a legitimate *skald*, if you will, is his deep immersion in the tradition and the profundity of his insight into it.

What exactly makes Wagner's appropriation of the Germanic myths so profound? In fact, what Wagner did was to weave together many different strands of the Germanic tradition (mythological, poetic, and philosophical) in order to create a *complete speech* laying bare the history and character of Western man. Wagner is the Hegel of music. The *Ring* is a kind of *phenomenology of the Western spirit*, expressed through the total work of art: combining drama, poetry, music, song, scenic design, costumes, and much else. In the *Ring* we confront ourselves and our *tragic* nature. For the *Ring* is a conscious and deliberate attempt on Wagner's part to create a modern equivalent of Greek tragedy. In the *Ring*, the tragic character is Western man himself. What is his tragic flaw? That is a point I will explore much later in this book.

As has already been implied by the foregoing, I will confine myself in the present text to the *Ring*, though a full consideration of Wagner's place in the Germanic tradition would obviously have to deal with most of his operas and their use of Germanic legend—including *Der fliegende Holländer, Tannhäuser, Lohen-*

*grin, Tristan und Isolde, Die Meistersinger von Nürnberg, Parsifal*, and various sketches for uncompleted works, such as *Wieland der Schmied*.

CHAPTER ONE:
# ORIGINS OF THE *RING*

The *Nibelungenlied*[1] was rediscovered in Germany in the early nineteenth century, in the wake of Romanticism and in the midst of the Napoleonic occupation. It was a time of increasing national awareness, and the *Nibelungenlied*, with its saga of the heroic Siegfried, was hailed as the great national epic. Dozens of editions were printed, both in modern German and in the original Middle High German, and it was taught in schools. By the 1830s the idea of adapting it into a grand opera had been floated by several authors. In 1853 composer Heinrich Dorn produced a *Nibelungen* opera, which enjoyed a certain popularity in Germany until it was completely eclipsed by Wagner's *Ring*. Germany in the early nineteenth century also saw a revival of interest in the old pagan Germanic gods, who soon took their place in schoolbooks alongside the Greek pantheon. It was into this milieu that Wagner was born (in 1813) and came of age. But it took him awhile to arrive at the idea of an opera based on Germanic myth.

Wagner was a German nationalist, though the nature of his nationalism was complex. To be a German nationalist in the nineteenth century meant that one advocated the unification of the German states (something that did not occur until 1871). Of course, German nationalism also consisted in German pride and celebration of all things German—sometimes, indeed,

---

[1] An anonymous epic poem in Middle High German, probably written between the period 1180 and 1210, telling the story of Siegfried.

to the point of extolling German superiority. But what always seems curious to us today is that this German nationalism often went hand in hand with an Enlightenment cosmopolitanism. The philosopher J. G. Fichte (1762-1814) is a paradigm case of this. He had long advocated such liberal ideals as the unification of mankind and the enlightenment of all peoples. During the Napoleonic occupation Fichte became an ardent nationalist, penning his famous *Addresses to the German Nation* (1808). But he had not fundamentally changed his ideals: it was Germany that would lead the way, Fichte believed, in unifying and enlightening mankind. Essentially, Wagner was cut from the same cloth.

Fichte had sought to awaken the German nation, to bring it to consciousness of itself, through his philosophy and the power of his rhetoric. Wagner set out to accomplish the same thing through opera — but first he had to reconceive opera itself. The model according to which he did so was Greek tragedy. Wagner believed that Greek tragedy was — up until his time — humanity's greatest artistic achievement. First, tragedy combined all the other arts: drama, poetry, mime, costumes, instrumental music, song, and dance. Most importantly, it was based upon myth, which was timeless and (so Wagner believed) revealed universal truths of human nature. The entire community participated in the tragedy, at least as spectators: when a tragedy was performed (always at state expense) it drew the entire populace. And since the tragedy was based on myth, the event had a religious significance.[2]

Wagner wrote the following in his essay *Art and*

---

[2] See Bryan Magee, *Aspects of Wagner* (Oxford: Oxford University Press, 1990), 5-6.

*Revolution*:

> With the Greeks the perfect work of art, the drama, was the sum and substance of all that could be expressed in the Greek nature; it was — in intimate connection with its history — the nation itself that stood facing itself in the work of art, becoming conscious of itself, and, in the space of a few hours, rapturously devouring, as it were, its own essence.[3]

Following the philosopher Ludwig Feuerbach (about whom I will have more to say later on), Wagner held that myth itself is a projection of the nature of a people, a people confronting itself. And it was essentially this thesis that led him to conceive the idea of an opera based upon the *Nibelungenlied* — though, as we shall see, Wagner's conception soon expanded beyond German legend to embrace Scandinavian myth as well. This made it much broader than merely "German." Indeed, though Wagner hoped through the *Ring* to bring Germany to consciousness of itself, his aim was actually much more ambitious than this: he hoped to awaken all of mankind, to express in his work universal truths of the human condition. Wagner wrote in *Art and Revolution*:

> If the Greek artwork embraced the spirit of a fine nation, the artwork of the future must embrace the spirit of free mankind, beyond all the confines of nationality; the national essence in it must be only an ornament, the charm of an in-

---

[3] Quoted in Bryan Magee, *The Tristan Chord: Wagner and Philosophy* (New York: Henry Holt and Company, 2000), 86-87.

dividual case amidst a multiplicity, and not a limiting barrier.

And, in *The Artwork of the Future*:

> Two main stages in the development of mankind lie clearly before us in history—the racial-national and the unnational-universal. If we are at present looking to the future for the completion of this second stage, we have in the past the closure of the first stage clearly discernible before our eyes.[4]

These lines may disappoint some. But it is important to keep in mind my earlier remarks, to the effect that Wagner's cosmopolitanism did not actually preclude his being a nationalist of a certain kind. It is equally important to keep in mind that these lines were written in 1848 and 1849, at a time when Wagner was an enthusiastic anarchist revolutionary and a friend of Mikhail Bakunin (1814–1876). However, as we shall see, in time Wagner abandoned his revolutionary ideals. It is safe to say that eventually he settled for awakening the German nation.

So, let us now consider exactly how the *Ring* was conceived and how it took shape. Wagner's original idea was to adapt the *Nibelungenlied* into a single opera titled *Siegfrieds Tod* (*Siegfried's Death*), which, as its title implies, would have concentrated on the events leading up to Siegfried's murder by the Burgundians (or Gibichungs). On October 4, 1848, four days prior to starting work on the libretto of *Siegfrieds Tod*, Wagner wrote a short "prose sketch" of the opera.

---

[4] Both quotes appear in Cooke on p. 264.

However, it went considerably beyond the material in the *Nibelungenlied*, creating an entirely new "back story" leading up to Siegfried's death, culled primarily from Wagner's study of Scandinavian mythology, and from scholarly attempts to reconstruct pre-Christian German myth. In this sketch we find the basic outlines of *Der Ring des Nibelungen*.

Wagner's intention was that the "back story" could be conveyed through dialogue (a device he employs in several of his works). However, he soon realized that the back story he had created was so elaborate that this was really impractical. And so he conceived the idea of writing not just one opera but a trilogy — a trilogy, that is to say, with a "prologue." In short, he conceived the idea of a tetralogy, though Wagner steadfastly insisted on referring to it as a trilogy with a prologue (*Das Rheingold*).

The timeline for the creation of the *Ring* is simple. Wagner wrote the libretti for *Das Rheingold* and *Die Walküre* in 1852 and completed the libretti for *Siegfried* and *Götterdämmerung* in 1853. In the autumn of that same year he began the music for *Das Rheingold* and finished it in January of 1854. The music of *Die Walküre* was begun in June 1854 and finished late in the fall. Then there is a gap, with work on *Siegfried* not beginning until 1857. Wagner finished the first act in April but then interrupted it in order to write *Tristan und Isolde*, at the behest of the Bavarian King Ludwig II, who had become Wagner's chief patron. The music for the second act of *Siegfried* was not written until June 1865, and the third act was finished in early 1869. The music of *Götterdämmerung* was begun the following year but not completed until 1874.

I turn now to the topic which will probably be of greatest interest to my readers: Wagner's use of the mythic German and Scandinavian sources. There are five major primary sources for the *Ring* (as opposed to secondary scholarly sources). The first, of course, has already been mentioned: the thirteenth-century *Nibelungenlied*. This is, in fact, the only one of Wagner's primary sources in (Middle High) German. It was written by an unknown author in Austria, four centuries after the Christian conversion.

The Christian elements in the poem bothered Wagner, as did the medieval courtly refinement that the anonymous author took such obvious pleasure in describing. Wagner wanted a rougher, more barbaric, pagan Siegfried, so he looked to the Scandinavian sources, which he believed were "more authentic." Thus, one of the effects of Wagner's appropriation of the story of Siegfried in the *Nibelungenlied* is to strip it of Christian accretions and to return it to its (probably) pre-Christian, pagan context. Wagner would later write:

> My studies drew me on, through the poems of the middle ages, right back to the foundations of the ancient German mythology; I was able to strip away one distorting veil after another which later poetry had thrown over it, and so set eyes on it at last in all its chaste beauty. . . . Although the splendid figure of Siegfried had long attracted me, he only fully enthralled me for the first time when I succeeded in freeing him from all his later trappings and saw him before me in his purest human form. It was then for the first time too, that I recognized the possibility of making him the hero of a drama, which had never occurred to me while I knew him only

from the medieval *Nibelungenlied*.[5]

Among the four major Scandinavian sources, the first that must be mentioned is *Thidreks saga*, another thirteenth-century text, compiled in Norway in Old Norse. It is believed to be based upon German materials—indeed scholars believe that all of the Scandinavian sources dealing with Siegfried (Sigurd) are elaborations of German sources. (To avoid confusion I will use the Wagnerian form "Siegfried" and other Wagnerian versions of traditional names throughout this book—hence Siegfried, not Sigurd; Brünnhilde not Brynhild, etc.)

This means that Wagner's belief that the Scandinavian sources presented a more "authentic" Siegfried is probably erroneous. (Though it is still possible, one supposes, that there could have been some very ancient tradition that both the German and Scandinavian sources drew upon.) *Thidreks saga* primarily deals with Dietrich von Bern, but also includes stories concerning Siegfried, the Nibelungs, and Attila the Hun (who figures in the *Nibelungenlied* as King Etzel).

The other three primary sources were all compiled between 1150 and 1270 in Iceland (which had a late conversion to Christianity, around 1000). First is the *Poetic Edda*, from which Wagner drew details about the gods and Siegfried. Second is the *Prose Edda*, which contains some myths that Wagner adapted, as well as a fairly lengthy sketch of the Siegfried legend. Finally, the *Volsunga saga* was Wagner's most important source of all, in which he found woven together almost all the elements he needed for the *Ring*, told with a great wealth of detail.

---

[5] Quoted in Cooke, 98.

In addition to these five sources, Wagner made some limited use of a few others. These include *Nornagests thattr* (or the *Story of Norna-Gest*) a fourteenth-century Scandinavian text that summarized the Siegfried story, with some original details. Two other minor sources include the fifteenth-century *Heldenbuch* (*Book of Heroes*), and the sixteenth-century *Lied vom hürnen Seyfrid* (*Song of the Horny Siegfried*, "horny" referring to his skin, impervious to attack—except, of course, in one spot).

We know from Wagner's correspondence that he consulted all of the above-mentioned texts. Also, all are in his Dresden library (which has been preserved) with the exception of *Thidreks saga*, *Volsunga saga*, and *Nornagests thattr*. Wagner had difficulty locating the *Volsunga saga* but finally was able to consult a copy in the Dresden Royal Library in October 1848. He studied German translations of all the Scandinavian texts. However, we also know that he actually did look at the Old Norse originals, studying them side by side with the available translations. Wagner's personal library contains two translations of the *Prose Edda* and translations of portions of the *Poetic Edda*. He borrowed more translations of the *Poetic Edda* from the Royal Library. (A complete German translation did not appear until 1851.)

In addition to the above primary sources, Wagner was also heavily indebted to the scholarly literature on the German and Scandinavian texts. The field of "German studies" had emerged largely as a result of the Romantic movement, and the first serious philological work on the medieval sources was being produced around the time of Wagner's birth. In researching the *Ring*, Wagner read *virtually all* this scholarship. Particularly important to him, however, were two works by the Brothers Grimm: Wilhelm's *Die Deutsche Heldensage*, published in 1829, and Jacob's *Deutsche Mythologie*, which appeared in 1835.

The Grimms were engaged in a common scholarly task: to reconstruct the ancient, pre-Christian German faith and traditions. In Scandinavia, pagan beliefs had been preserved in the *Eddas* and sagas, but no comparable German texts existed. The Grimms reasoned that traces of the old German religion had to have been preserved in such sources as folktales, place names, and Christian demonologies. Wilhelm and Jacob scoured every possible source, attempting to piece together a reasonable picture of what the old religion must have been like. (In the process, they collected their volume of *Märchen*, or fairy tales, the achievement for which they are now best known to the public.) As a kind of model on which to base their reconstruction, the Grimms looked to Scandinavian mythology, reasoning that it was a local inflection of a mythology common to all the Germanic tribes.

It would be no exaggeration to say that Wagner was almost as inspired by the Grimms' scholarship as he was by the primary sources. Countless elements in the *Ring* have their origin in Wagner's study of the two aforementioned books by the Grimms. Jacob Grimm had established *Wuotan* as the name of the chief German god, mentioning also a Saxon variant *Wôdan*. Wagner's initial choice for the name of the chief god of the *Ring* (really, its main character) was Wôdan, but after a while he changed it to *Wotan*, adapted from Grimm's Wuotan. (Grimm does not actually give the form "Wotan.") The following chart summarizes Grimm's list of the "reconstructed" names of German gods and Wagner's alterations to them:

| GRIMM | WAGNER |
|---|---|
| Wuotan | Wotan |
| Frikka | Fricka |
| Frouwa | Freia |
| Donar | Donner |
| Frô | Froh |

The Grimms often made imaginative links between names and other elements in the sources they utilized, and this seems to have emboldened Wagner to do the same—achieving a kind of fusion of German and Scandinavian elements. Indeed, some of the inferences or connections for which Wagner has been criticized actually have their origin with the Grimms. For example, Wagner also includes a character named "Loge," who is the equivalent of the Scandinavian Loki. In fact, there is scant evidence that there was a Loki figure in the German mythological world. However, Jacob Grimm postulated "Locho" or "Loho" as possible German equivalents. Wagner didn't particularly like either and settled on "Loge."

Purists have long railed against Wagner, however, for making his Loge/Loki a god of fire. Again, however, this has its origin in Grimm. In Scandinavian myth there was a fire giant named Logi, and Grimm thought that there might be a connection to Loki. (More recent scholarship doesn't support this.) We find the origin of Wagner's Loge in these words of Jacob Grimm: "Now a striking narrative . . . places *Logi* by the side of *Loki*: a being from the giant province beside a kinsman and companion of the gods. This is no mere play upon words, the two really signify the same thing from different points of view, *Logi* the natural force of fire, and *Loki* with a shifting of the sound, a shifting of the sense: of the burly giant has been made a sly, seducing villain."[6]

Wagner's "Erda" also comes from Jacob Grimm, who postulated her as the equivalent of the "earth goddess" Nerthus mentioned by Tacitus in his *Germania*. Unfortunately, Grimm could not turn up any evidence that the German Wuotan possessed any of the personal characteristics familiar to us from Wagner: his one eye, his spear, his guise as the "wanderer," etc. Wagner simply borrows all of this from the Scandinavian sources. In doing this he was, however, merely following the example of the Grimms in using the Scandinavian materials as a touchstone for reconstructing German beliefs. (Though in this case and in others, he allowed himself the sort of license permitted to an artist but forbidden to a scholar.)

Let us turn now to consider another issue: the literary form of the *Ring*. My readers may be surprised to learn that in the *Ring* (and in none of his other works) Wagner made use of an ancient Germanic form of alliterative verse called *Stabreim*. This was the verse form of, among other texts, the *Poetic Edda* and *Beowulf*. Deryck Cooke gives the following succinct description of Stabreim: "a line of four stresses, divided into two symmetrical halves of two stresses each, and having either two or three of the stresses emphasized by using the same initial sound for the different words (all vowels counting the same)."[7] Cooke uses the following example to compare Wagner's use of *Stabreim* to that of the *Poetic Edda*. This example also illustrates how Wagner drew direct inspiration from the words

---

[6] Jacob Grimm, *Teutonic Mythology*, vol. 1, trans. James Steven Stallybrass (Mineola, NY: Dover Publications, 2004), 241.

[7] Cooke, 74.

of the *Edda*, not just its literary form. In both instances, it is Brünnhilde who speaks, having just been awakened by Siegfried:

*Poetic Edd*a (*Sigrdrifumal*, The Lay of Sigrdrifa):

Heill dagr! Heilir dags synir!
Heil *n*ótt ok *n*ipt!
Óreiþom *a*ugom litið okkr þinig
Ok gefið sitjǫndum *s*igr!

(Hail to the day! Hail to the sons of day!
Hail to night and her kin!
With gracious eyes may you look upon us,
And give victory to those sitting here!<sup>8</sup>)

Wagner, *Siegfried*, Act Three, Scene Three:

Heil dir, Sonne! Heil dir, Licht!
Heil dir, *l*euchtender Tag!
Lang' war mein Schlaf; ich bin er*w*acht:
*W*er ist der Held, der mich er*w*eckt'?

(Hail to you, sun! Hail to you, light!
Hail to you, light-bringing day!
Long was my sleep, awakened am I:
Who is the hero who woke me?[9])

---

[8] The translation appears in *The Poetic Edda*, trans. Carolyne Larrington (Oxford: Oxford University Press, 1996), 167.

[9] The translation is in *Wagner's Ring of the Nibelung: A Companion*, ed. Stewart Spencer and Barry Millington, libretti translated by Stewart Spencer [henceforth: Spencer] (New York: Thames and Hudson, 1993), 267.

The form is not identical, and Wagner does take some liberties—but, as Cooke notes, the effect is the same. The *Nibelungenlied*, it should be noted, did not employ Stabreim but was written instead in the then-fashionable style of "end rhyme," with rhyming couplets. Thus, we are faced with the interesting fact that in its verse style Wagner's *Ring* is more traditional, more *urdeutsch* than the *Nibelungenlied*.

In Chapter Three I will discuss in detail how Wagner made use of the source material mentioned earlier. But before turning to the full story of how Wagner wove together all these different strands to create the *Ring*, let's anticipate and respond to some objections against what he produced. We have now seen that Wagner was deeply immersed in the sources and conversant with most of the major scholarly literature on the subject. But, some will say, why did he have to "distort" those sources? Why did he have to graft myths onto one another and change them? And, worse yet, why did he have to invent wholly new material? Weren't the canonical stories enough for him?

In responding to these sorts of objections, let's consider first that Wagner's project of achieving a synthesis of Germanic myth was not original with him. It was also the project of the anonymous author of the *Nibelungenlied*. As Cooke notes, writing of that author, "His work eclipsed the previous materials because he had the masterly idea of conflating them into a large, comprehensive epic, and the genius to carry out this idea by expanding and reshaping them in a way of his own."[10] But the exact same thing could be said of Wagner. And so, as Cooke also points out, if we must accuse Wagner of distortion then the author of the *Ni-*

---

[10] Cooke, 95.

*belungenlied* must stand accused as well.

But I can imagine some purists biting this bullet and declaring that the *Nibelungenlied*, with its courtly, Christian veneer is indeed a distortion. The trouble is that, for quite different reasons, the same accusation could be made against the *Volsunga saga*. The simple reason is that, as alluded to earlier, all the Scandinavian accounts of the Siegfried legend are now thought to be developments and elaborations of German originals. (This is why, again, Wagner's belief that in going to the Scandinavian material he was getting a "more authentic" Siegfried is problematic.) And, of course, if one compares the accounts of Siegfried in the *Volsunga saga*, *Poetic Edda*, *Prose Edda*, *Nornagests thattr*, and other sources, one will find that they differ with each other as much as do Matthew, Mark, Luke, and John.

It is completely pointless to debate which is the "authentic" story. Perhaps there was some great ur-text from which all of these, ultimately, are drawn. But if so, it has been lost to us. Such possibilities, however, are really beside the point. Each of these texts is an artistic creation. They are not self-effacing attempts to faithfully mirror some original source. That would, in fact, be contrary to the Germanic spirit. No, they are highly *individual* creations, using the basic Siegfried story as a framework which they then embellish and elaborate, often intermingling it with other myths and heroic legends.

Cooke says it best: "Each source, in fact, represents a new artistic interpretation of pre-existing material, to suit the writer's purpose; and *The Ring* is a comprehensive artistic interpretation of the whole main essence of the material, undertaken by one of the greatest imaginations in human history." And furthermore, Cooke expresses my own view when he says, "It might even be argued that *The Ring* is as valid and coherent a dramatic synthesis of the complex mythology of Northern Europe as we are ever likely to get."[11]

At the same time, however, it must be noted that Wagner's *Ring* is not just a "synthesis" of Germanic mythology. Wagner's purpose was to use that mythology to convey a message—initially about the state of the modern world, then, later on, about the state of life itself. But here the critics will pounce: "You see, Wagner distorts the myths by using them to convey his own ideas!" But should we suppose that the authors of the *Nibelungenlied*, *Volsunga saga*, and other texts, were really doing anything different? They too were recasting pre-existing material in order to speak to their own time—and to reveal truths that are timeless and universal. This was exactly Wagner's own aim.

Wagner wrote the following in *Opera and Drama*: "The incomparable thing about myth is that it is true for all time, and its content, however closely compressed, is inexhaustible throughout the ages. The only task of the poet is to expound it."[12] Of course, our imaginary objectors might still argue that perhaps the ideas that Wagner expresses through the myths distort the spirit of the myths themselves. This is a much more difficult issue to address, but I will do my best to address it in Chapter Four. For now, I will simply say that I believe a convincing case can be made, as Cooke puts it, that the *Ring* is "a justifiable interpretation of latent implications in the original material."[13] Further, as I have said already, I believe that the myths have the power to possess whoever takes them up, and to

---

[11] Cooke, both quotes appear on p. 86.
[12] Quoted in Cooke, 87.
[13] Cooke, 86.

shape his outlook and take it in new directions. I believe this was the case with Wagner—whose change in outlook while writing the *Ring* cannot be attributed entirely to Schopenhauer. There is something about these myths and legends that resonates deeply with anyone of Germanic ancestry. It unlocks something inside them. And in Wagner's case, it helped him give birth to one of the greatest creations of the Western spirit.

## Chapter Two:
# The Story of
# *Der Ring des Nibelungen*

For the uninitiated, I will now tell the story of the *Ring*, confining myself to essentials. Even the initiated would do well to read this summary, just to refamiliarize themselves with the story, as the account of Wagner's use of the source material to follow will presuppose that one is well-acquainted with the events of all four operas. Those who feel they are very familiar with the storyline of the *Ring* can skip to the next chapter.

*Das Rheingold* begins deep beneath the surface of the river Rhine. Three mermaids, or water nymphs ("Rhine Daughters") guard a chunk of gold that possesses special properties: using a magic spell, it can be shaped into a ring that would confer on its wearer mastery over the entire earth. However, there's a catch: the spell can only be worked by one who has completely renounced love. The dwarf Alberich appears and desperately tries to woo the Rhine daughters. After they mercilessly taunt the ugly creature, he renounces love and steals the gold.

Meanwhile, on a nearby mountain, Wotan and the gods are waiting to take possession of Valhalla, which is being built for them by a pair of giants. Egged on by the mischievous Loge, Wotan has made an unwise deal with them: he has promised the giants the beautiful Freia as payment, should they complete the job on time. Wotan fully expects to be able to get out of this deal, on some pretext or other. But when the giants finish the job and show up expecting payment, he is at a loss to know what to do. He can't give up Freia, as she is the source of the golden apples that keep the gods eternally young.

Once more coming to Wotan's aid, Loge tells him of how Alberich has acquired the ring of power and is busy amassing a treasure with the aid of the Nibelungs (dwarfs), who are now his serfs. Wotan and Loge descend into Nibelheim in order to steal the treasure from Alberich and offer it to the giants as substitute for Freia (an arrangement the giants tentatively accept). In Nibelheim, Alberich brags of his powers and demonstrates his newly-created Tarnhelm, a kind of cap that can make its wearer invisible, or allow him to take any shape he wishes. Loge tricks Alberich into taking the shape of a tiny frog — whereupon Loge and Wotan nab the evil dwarf and return to the surface of the earth with both him and his treasure.

Wotan forces Alberich to give up the ring of power and puts it on his own hand. But Alberich isn't going to go quietly: he curses the ring, promising that all who wear it will meet their doom. The giants, whose names are Fasolt and Fafner, are pleased with Wotan's compromise and claim the treasure and the Tarnhelm. Suddenly, however, wise Erda (a kind of chthonic goddess-prophetess) rises from the earth and advises Wotan to shun the ring. He wants to gain more knowledge from her, but she disappears quickly. Having now heard of the Ring's powers, the giants demand it as well, and Wotan has no choice but to relinquish his prize. But the curse soon shows its power when Fafner kills Fasolt in a quarrel over possession of the ring. Remorselessly, the dull-witted Fafner lumbers off with ring, Tarnhelm, and treasure. Satisfied that Freia is safe, the gods cause a rainbow bridge to appear and walk across it, entering Valhalla. They leave behind clever Loge, who predicts their downfall.

When *Die Walküre* begins, many years have passed since the events just described. Wotan fears the power of the ring, now in the hands of Fafner, and at the same time he covets it. So, he has hatched a two-part scheme. First, he has descended into the earth and ravished Erda, siring on her nine immortal, semi-divine female warriors: the Valkyries. It is their job to gather dead heroes and bear them to Valhalla. Wotan, in short, is building an army of the dead, who will be able to defend him against a possible onslaught by whoever may bear the ring. (Before losing the ring, Alberich had promised Wotan that he intended to storm Valhalla, and Fafner might well do the same.)

Second, in the guise of "Wälse" Wotan has sired twins on a mortal woman. Their names are Siegmund and Sieglinde. Siegmund is now a young man, and Wotan has guided him since infancy, hoping that he will become a hero capable of killing Fafner and capturing the ring—for immediate delivery to Wotan, needless to say. Why can't Wotan slay Fafner himself? Because his power rests upon the treaties and agreements he has made (all of which are engraved on his spear). If he reneged on his agreement with Fafner and killed him, his power would lose its legitimacy in the eyes of the world. Only a man—a hero—free of Wotan's entanglements may defeat Fafner and acquire the ring.

All of the above is, in fact, the background to *Die Walküre*, revealed entirely through dialogue. When the actual story opens, Siegmund is on the run, pursued by the vengeful clan of Hunding, whom he has wronged in some fashion. He seeks shelter in a house, not realizing that it is actually Hunding's own home. Fortunately, Hunding is out, and Siegmund is given hospitality by none other than Sieglinde, who is now Hunding's wife. The twins were separated when they were very young, however, and do not immediately recognize each other. When Hunding returns, he informs Siegmund that the next day they will fight a duel to the death. Then he retires, leaving the twins alone. Slowly, they come to recognize each other—and simultaneously to feel something more than just familial love. Siegmund tells his sister that their father, Wälse (Wotan), had promised him a sword in his hour of direst need. And, lo and behold, Sieglinde shows him a sword thrust into a great ash tree that stands at the center of the house. It was put there long ago by Wotan in his guise as the grey-bearded Wanderer. Siegmund draws the sword from the tree and christens it Nothung ("needful"). Then he claims Sieglinde as his bride, and the two of them disappear into the forest.

Meanwhile, on a barren mountainside, Fricka is in high dudgeon over Siegmund and Sieglinde's adultery, to say nothing of their incest. Fricka, you see, is the goddess of hearth and home, so she takes the forbidden love of the twins as an affront to her authority. And she knows everything about Wotan's little scheme. She confronts her weary husband, demanding that when Siegmund faces Hunding, Siegmund must die. This, of course, is the very last thing Wotan wants, since his plan is that Siegmund must go on to win the ring. But Fricka also confronts Wotan with his own self-deception: Siegmund is no "free hero"; Wotan has manipulated him every step of the way. Seeing the truth of it, the Lord of Hosts has no choice but to give in to her demands.

After Fricka departs, Wotan is comforted by his favorite Valkyrie, Brünnhilde. He confesses everything to her, including his lust for the ring's terrible power. But now, in a state of extreme dejection, he admits that all he longs for is "the end." He orders Brünnhilde to go to Siegmund and insure that on the following day he will fall to Hunding's sword. Brünnhilde is stunned, as she knows of Wotan's love for Siegmund. But she reluctantly agrees to do as he has commanded her.

After Brünnhilde meets Siegmund, however, and hears of his deep love for Sieglinde (he refuses to enter Valhalla without her) she decides that she cannot carry out Wotan's orders. Besides, she has the capacity to see into Wotan's heart, and reads there his true desire: that Siegmund should live. So when the battle with Hunding begins, Brünnhilde defies Wotan and attempts to defend Siegmund. Suddenly, however, Wotan himself appears, shatters Siegmund's sword with his spear, and allows Hunding to kill his beloved son. Brünnhilde quickly manages to gather the fragments of the sword and disappears with Sieglinde—who by this point is pregnant with Siegmund's child: the greatest hero of them all, Siegfried.

Riding her horse Grane, Brünnhilde carries Sieglinde to a mountaintop where the other Valkyries are gathered and implores them to help her. Terrified of Wotan's wrath, they make a token attempt to conceal Brünnhilde when the god finally arrives, bent on punishing his favorite. Sieglinde hastens away, carrying the fragments of Nothung, and Wotan pronounces his judgment: Brünnhilde is to be rendered mortal, then put to sleep. She must take as husband the first man to waken her, even if he is the lowliest man on earth. Brünnhilde defends herself, stating that she only did what she knew Wotan truly wanted, in his heart of hearts. He knows that this is true, and his love for her moves him to grant Brünnhilde's one request: that her slumbering body be encircled by flames that only a hero can pass through. (We all know who that hero will be—and so, it seems, do Wotan and Brünnhilde.) Wotan puts her to sleep and summons Loge, the god of fire, to ring her with a wall of flame.

Perhaps close to twenty years have passed when *Siegfried* begins, for the title character is now a young man. His mother, Sieglinde, died giving birth to him, and he has been raised all these years by the dwarf Mime. This is no kindly foster father, however. He is the brother of Alberich and longs to gain the ring for himself. He has raised Siegfried just so that he might grow up, kill Fafner, and hand the ring over to him. (In short, not unlike how Wotan raised Siegmund!) Such a task will require a great hero, for in the intervening years Fafner has changed himself into a dragon (presumably by means of the Tarnhelm, though Wagner does not say so). He now guards the ring and the treasure in a cave deep in the forest.[1] Mime has told Siegfried nothing of his parentage, insisting that he is both the boy's father and mother. But the young hero has grown to hate the scheming Mime and is physically repulsed by him—sensing intuitively that he cannot be the dwarf's son. Mime, for his part, hates Siegfried for his beauty and purity and sees him only as a tool.

When Mime found the dying Sieglinde, not only did he spirit away her child, but also the fragments of

---

[1] An alternative hypothesis is that possession of the ring has physically corrupted Fafner, as it does Smeagol in Tolkien's *Lord of the Rings*. Rather than use the obvious modern German word *Drache*, Wagner deliberately employs the Old High German *Wurm*. This meant the same thing as "dragon," but the image it conveys is of something larval rather than reptilian.

Nothung. Since then, the dwarf has tried repeatedly to reforge the sword, without success. Wotan, in his guise as the Wanderer, comes knocking one day while Siegfried is out. He challenges Mime to a guessing game, and the price if Mime loses will be his head! The question and answer session that follows becomes an opportunity for Wagner to remind the audience of what has occurred in the preceding two operas. Mime loses, but Wotan lets him keep his head—and even gives him some advice: only a man who has never felt fear may forge the sword and make it whole again. Then he departs.

Wotan, of course, has described Siegfried. And lately, in fact, Siegfried has been perplexed over the fact that he has yet to experience this "fear" that Mime speaks of now and then. When he returns home, he forces Mime to reveal the truth about his parents. Then he seizes the fragments of Nothung and successfully reforges the sword. While Siegfried is at the fiery forge, a jubilant Mime plots to kill the boy as soon as he has slain Fafner. He is now more convinced than ever that the ring will soon be his.

A little later, Wotan encounters Alberich in the forest. The unhappy dwarf is lingering about outside Fafner's cave. Together, they rouse Fafner from his slumber and warn him that a hero approaches who may be his undoing. But the dragon dismisses their words and slumbers on, sitting atop his hoard. The god and the dwarf depart, and soon Mime and Siegfried arrive at the mouth of the cave. The dragon attacks Siegfried, who uses Nothung to deal him a mortal blow. Before Fafner dies, however, he warns an uncomprehending Siegfried that there is a curse on the treasure. When Siegfried burns his fingers on the dragon's corrosive blood, he involuntarily sucks on them—and is suddenly able to understand the language of the birds calling to him from the trees. A bird warns Siegfried that Mime intends to poison him. Having now had quite enough of the nosy old dwarf, Siegfried runs him through with the sword. The bird also advises Siegfried as to the location of a certain maiden, asleep on a mountaintop ringed by fire. Taking the ring and Tarnhelm, Siegfried sets off to rescue Brünnhilde.

At the base of the mountain on which the Valkyrie sleeps, Wotan raises Erda from the earth to question her about the fate of the gods. She has no more to tell him than he already knows: the age of the gods is nearing its end. Resigned to his fate, Wotan expresses the hope that together Siegfried and Brünnhilde will redeem the world. However, when he actually crosses paths with Siegfried later on, Wotan is suddenly seized again by the desire to hold on to his power. He attempts to block Siegfried's way, but the hero (who has never learned of the gods) shatters Wotan's spear (the symbol of his power) with Nothung. Immediately, Wotan disappears—and never appears again in the *Ring*. Siegfried successfully passes through the fiery barrier and finds Brünnhilde in full armor. At first, he thinks she must be a man. But when he removes the armor he realizes otherwise—and for the first time in his life feels fear. Brünnhilde awakes joyfully but then realizes to her horror that she is now a mortal woman. Soon, however, the two find themselves in love. With an outpouring of jubilation, they celebrate their love—and the twilight of the gods.

*Götterdämmerung* opens with a prologue involving the three Norns. Together they spin the fates of man, represented by a great thread. The three sisters recount the tale of how, at the beginning of time, Wotan gave up his eye to drink at their well of wisdom, and of how he tore a branch from the world ash tree to serve as his spear. But since then the well has dried up, and the tree has never recovered from this violation: it has withered and died. The Norns tell us that Wotan, having now lost his worldly power to Siegfried, has ordered the dead heroes of Valhalla to cut up the tree and pile the wood around his fortress. It will not be long before the god will thrust one end of his shattered spear into Loge, whereupon fire will consume Valhalla and the entire world. As to the events that will follow, the Norns are uncertain. Suddenly, as they gather the thread, it snaps. The end of time is near.

At the opening of Act One, the scene shifts to the Hall of the Gibichungs (Burgundians) on the Rhine. The Gibichung king is Gunther, a weak and vacillating man. His most trusted advisor is the dour Hagen, his half-brother, who is actually the son of Alberich. Just as Wotan sired Siegmund in order to acquire the ring, Alberich sired Hagen for the same task. Gunther is seeking a suitable wife, and Hagen now advises him that he should use Siegfried to win Brünnhilde for himself and make her his queen. Once that task is done, Siegfried can marry Gunther's sister, Gutrune. Of course, all of this is really a scheme on Hagen's part to acquire the ring.

As luck would have it, Siegfried arrives a little later, having left Brünnhilde on her mountaintop to go adventuring. Before leaving her, however, he gave her the cursed ring as a token of his love. On his arrival at the Gibichung court, Siegfried is given a magic potion that makes him lose all memory of Brünnhilde—and immediately fall in love with Gutrune. After Siegfried and Gunther become blood brothers, the hero agrees to don the Tarnhelm, taking on Gunther's likeness, and to pass through the flames and win Brünnhilde for the Gibichung king.

Meanwhile, Brünnhilde is visited on her lonely mountaintop by Waltraute, another of the Valkyries. She pleads with Brünnhilde to restore the ring to the Rhine. Waltraute tells her of Wotan, who now sits in Valhalla in a state of profound depression, awaiting the end of the world. Only Brünnhilde may now avert the coming catastrophe if she will restore the natural order of things and return the ring to the Rhine daughters. But Brünnhilde refuses to part with the ring, since Siegfried gave it to her as a sign of his love. Almost as soon as Waltraute leaves, Siegfried himself appears—but, of course, he is a changed man (in more than one sense). He seizes the ring from Brünnhilde's hand and declares her the property of King Gunther. Of course, the confused Brünnhilde really believes that he is Gunther, as Siegfried is wearing the Tarnhelm. Later, he will turn her over to the real king, and then travel separately, back to the Gibichung palace on the Rhine.

When Gunther and Brünnhilde arrive at the Gibichung court, they are greeted by Hagen and by Gunther's vassals. And, of course, by Siegfried. Brünnhilde is astonished to see him there and to hear that he is engaged to Gutrune. Siegfried, of course, has no memory of her. Brünnhilde swears an oath that she and Siegfried have lain together as man and wife. Speaking falsely, but honestly, Siegfried insists that they have not, and then departs. Left alone with Brünnhilde and Gunther, Hagen offers to avenge her by killing Siegfried, and Brünnhilde reveals the one vulnerable spot on the hero's body: his back. In Wagner's version this is not because the dragon's blood missed a spot. It is because Brünnhilde did not protect Siegfried's back with her magic spells, thinking it unnecessary since Siegfried would never turn his back on an opponent. (What she fails to realize, of course, is that the world now contains men without honor, who would gladly stab the hero in the back—a significant point, to which we will return.) For his part, Gunther agrees to the plot against Siegfried, believing that he may well have lain with Brünnhilde. Under these unhappy circumstances, the double wedding nevertheless proceeds.

The plan is to kill Siegfried while he, Gunther, and Hagen are off in the forest hunting. On the appointed day, Siegfried finds himself confronted by the three Rhine daughters. They implore him to return the ring, telling him that it is cursed. Foolishly, he ignores their pleas. Hagen then gives Siegfried an antidote to the magic potion he took earlier. The hero begins to remember everything—and just as he recollects his love for Brünnhilde, Hagen stabs him in the back. The hunting party then carries Siegfried's lifeless body back to the castle. Gutrune is beside herself with sorrow, accusing her brother of murder. But Hagen brazenly takes credit for the deed. When Hagen and Gunther quarrel over the ring, Hagen kills his king. But when he reaches down to take the ring from Siegfried's finger, he is horrified when the dead man raises his arm threateningly.

Brünnhilde orders a funeral pyre to be built for Siegfried. She proclaims that Siegfried's death has atoned for Wotan's guilt and that her suffering has at last made her wise. She command's Wotan's ravens to return to Valhala, bringing him news of the world's imminent demise. Taking the ring, Brünnhilde promises that it will be returned to the Rhine. Then she ignites the funeral pyre and, mounting Grane, rides into the flames. The castle is consumed in fire, and the Rhine overflows its banks. Hagen is still bent on capturing the ring, but the Rhine daughters drag him into the water to his death. Soon the entire world has caught fire, and we see Valhalla itself consumed in flames. The gods are no more. But the orchestra returns to the "Rhine music" heard at the very beginning of the *Ring*, suggesting rebirth, and eternal cycles of creation and destruction.

## Chapter Three:
# Wagner's Sources

As a brief summary of how Wagner makes use of the major sources discussed in Chapter One, I don't think one could do any better than this paragraph from an article by Elizabeth Magee:

> Looking back, we can see how the *Eddas* supplied most of *Das Rheingold*, aided by a view of the Nibelungs taken from *Das Lied vom hürnen Seyfrid*. The *Volsunga saga*, supplemented by skaldic poetry, dominates *Die Walküre*. *Siegfried* retains the Wanderer from the *Volsunga Saga* and introduces the *Thidreks saga* boyhood tale into an *Edda*-based scenario. In *Götterdämmerung* Wagner blends *Edda* and *Volsunga saga* material until finally, at Siegfried's death, the German *Nibelungenlied* is allowed to come into its own. The perishing of the gods of the epilogue and the purging by fire and flood bring us back to the *Snorra Edda* and the *Völuspá*.[1]

Of course, there's a great deal more to tell—and it is a rather intricate story. Still, a full study of Wagner's adaptation of the sources would take a book unto itself, so we can only scratch the surface here.

First of all, let us note that the stories of Siegfried do not originate, as Wagner supposed, in Scandinavia. In fact, the earliest sources are thought to be Frankish and Burgundian lays, written as late as the fifth centu-

---

[1] Elizabeth Magee, "In Pursuit of the Purely Human: The 'Ring' and its Medieval Sources," in Spencer, 32.

ry. These somehow or other made their way to Scandinavia and were elaborated in the *Volsunga saga* and other texts. There is nothing in the German materials (including the *Nibelungenlied*) about the ring, Brünnhilde being a Valkyrie, Siegfried and Brünnhilde meeting prior to his encountering Gutrune (Kriemhild), a magic potion that makes him forget Brünnhilde, and many other details. In fact, there is nothing in the German accounts of Siegfried even about the gods. Wagner derived all of these elements from the Scandinavian sources.

It is rather ironic that most educated people believe that the *Ring* is based heavily upon the *Nibelungenlied*, when in fact Wagner derives comparatively little from it. Elizabeth Magee, in the passage quoted above, puts the matter quite correctly: it is only in *Götterdämmerung*, and then really only in the parts dealing with Siegfried's death, that Wagner is greatly indebted to the *Nibelungenlied*. As to the *Thidreks saga*, though it is in Old Norse it is thought to be mainly a translation of German materials, possibly a translation of a single German text. From *Thidreks saga*, Wagner derived the motif of Hagen ("Hogni") being only part human. In this text, his father is an elf; he shares his mother with Gunther. Furthermore, Wagner derived from *Thidreks saga* much of the material about Siegfried's boyhood: how he was raised by Mime the smith (here "Mimir"), his splitting of the anvil, etc. In *Thidreks saga* the dragon is actually Mimir's brother (called here "Regin," elsewhere the name of the smith who raises Siegfried). After dispatching "Regin," Siegfried kills Mimir/ Mime, just as in Wagner's version.

There is much more to tell about Wagner's use of the purely Scandinavian materials. First of all, in all three of the major Scandinavian sources Wagner utilized (the *Poetic Edda*, *Prose Edda*, and *Volsunga saga*) there occurs some version of the story of "Andvari's gold," which was extremely important to Wagner. In brief—and sticking closely to the version in the *Prose Edda*—Odin, Loki, and Hoenir are out exploring when Loki spies an otter who has just caught a salmon. Acting quickly, he kills the otter with a stone, bagging both him and the fish. But it turns out that the otter is the son of a powerful man named Hreithmar, who has two other sons: Fafnir and Regin. They capture the Aesir and skin Otter, demanding that the gods pay a ransom of gold great enough to cover the skin entirely. So Loki descends into the world of the "dark elves" (dwarfs) and finds a dwarf named Andvari who has amassed a large treasure by means of a ring that can magically produce gold (and this is all it does, by the way: it is not a ring of "power," in the sense of power over others). When Loki steals both the treasure and the ring, Andvari places a curse upon them. Odin at first wants to keep the ring for himself, but he has to relinquish it in order to completely cover Otter's skin. Fafnir and Regin then kill their father for the treasure, but Fafnir makes off with it, hoarding it on Gnita Heath and changing himself into a dragon. Regin then raises young Sigurd, who slays both Fafnir and Regin, etc.

It is obvious how this story forms the basic framework of the *Ring*, with a number of details changed. For example, the Aesir need the treasure in Wagner's version in order to ransom Freia. With that alteration, Wagner fuses the Andvari story with the story in the *Prose Edda* of the building of Valhalla, as well as the story of the theft of Idun's apples (about which I'll have more to say in a moment). Andvari becomes Alberich. Fafnir and Regin become Fafner and Fasolt, the giants who build Valhalla for the gods. Regin becomes Mime, who in Wagner's version is obviously no relation to Fafner. It is Freia that the treasure must cover, not Otter's skin. And, most important of all, the ring becomes a ring of power as well as a device for generating treasure. (One common misunderstanding of *Der Ring des Nibelungen* is that Alberich's treasure is the Rhinegold: in fact, the ring is the Rhinegold, whole and entire, in a transformed shape; the treasure is accumulated by means of the ring.)

Now as to Freia and her golden apples, this comes about in Wagner through conflating the figure of Freia with the goddess Idun. In the *Prose Edda* it is said that the goddess Idun "keeps in her box the apples the gods have to eat, when they grow old, to become young again, and so it will continue up to Ragnarok."[2] Wagner simply combines Freia with Idun. This is not by any means an unreasonable move on his part, and some have theorized that Idun is in fact an aspect of Freia.[3] That her apples are golden seems to have been a feature Wagner borrowed from the mythic Greek apples of the garden of Hesperides.

In both the *Prose Edda* and *Poetic Edda*, we find Brünnhilde depicted as a Valkyrie[4], an element that does not appear in any of the German sources. In the *Poetic Edda* (but not the *Prose Edda*) she is punished by Odin for taking the wrong side in a battle and put to sleep by him. In the *Prose Edda* (and in the *Volsunga saga*) Siegfried gives her Andvari's ring, just as Wag-

---

[2] Snorri Sturluson, *The Prose Edda*, trans. Jean I. Young (Berkeley: University of California Press, 1984), 54.

[3] See for example Richard North, *The Haustlǫng of Þjóðólfr of Hvinir* (London: Hisarlik Press, 1997), xiv.

[4] Though in the *Sigrdrifumal* she is referred to as Sigrdrifa.

ner has Siegfried give Alberich's ring to Brünnhilde in the Prologue of *Götterdämmerung*. Regin (Wagner's Mime) is not a dwarf in either the *Prose Edda* or the *Volsunga saga*. Wagner draws this detail from the *Poetic Edda*, though it is not clear that the "Regin" listed as a dwarf in *Völuspá* is the same Regin who appears as Siegfried's foster father.

Wagner also derives from *Völuspá* the basic character of Erda, who prophesies, as does the Völva (seeress), the end of the gods. As Cooke points out, Tacitus provided Wagner with some further inspiration here, as he notes that Nerthus (Grimm's Erda) "intervenes in the affairs of men."[5] Wagner also refers to Erda as "Wala" and "Urwala." This too comes from Jacob Grimm, who theorized that *Walawa* or *Wala* was the Old High German equivalent of Völva.

There is, of course, much else in the *Eddas* that inspired Wagner and that he made use of—too much to detail here. He was particularly taken, it seems, by the description in the *Prose Edda* of the dwarfs as like maggots that had "quickened" in the flesh of Ymir.[6] In his "Prose Sketch" of the *Ring* from 1848, he describes the Nibelungs as "like worms in a dead body."[7] As Cooke points out, Wagner also borrowed the flavor of a number of exchanges in the *Poetic Edda*. In the *Vafþruðnismal*, Odin engages in a question and answer game with a giant, his head being the price for losing the contest—similar to Wotan's contest with Mime in *Siegfried*. In *Grimnismal*, Odin and Frigg quarrel over

---

[5] Cooke, 227.

[6] *Prose Edda*, 41.

[7] Richard Wagner, "The Nibelungen-Myth as Sketch for a Drama," in *Pilgrimage to Beethoven and Other Essays*, trans. William Ashton Ellis (Lincoln: University of Nebraska Press, 1994), 301. (Henceforth "Sketch.")

two rival warriors, much as Wotan and Fricka do over Siegmund and Hunding in *Die Walküre*. In *Lokasenna*, Loki taunts the gods relentlessly, not unlike Loge does in *Das Rheingold*. Many other examples could be adduced, offering further confirmation (if any is needed at this point) of how close a reader Wagner was of the traditional sources.

We now turn to the *Volsunga saga*, which is without question the most important source for the *Ring*. This is a fascinating text, which demands multiple readings. It is as barbaric a tale as there ever was, filled with instances of shocking brutality and brimming with much that is simply bizarre. It demands an esoteric reading, which someday I plan to produce. We have the entire Siegfried story presented here, repeating much of the material contained in the *Eddas*, including the story of Andvari's ring. Thus, one often cannot say categorically that this element or that was drawn by Wagner from the *Volsunga saga*, rather than from the *Eddas*. However, it is safe to say that the *Volsunga saga* was his major source and inspiration, as generally speaking it elaborates all elements of the Siegfried story in much greater detail than do the *Eddas*.

It is only in the *Volsunga saga* that we have the full account of Siegfried's parentage. Indeed, several generations pass in the story before Siegfried ever appears. In the *Volsunga saga*, Siegfried is not produced through an incestuous union of brother and sister. The product of that union, in fact, is Sinfjotli, whose sibling parents are Siegmund and Signy. Siegfried is actually the son of Siegmund and his third wife, Hjordis. However, Wagner wisely considered the motif of the incestuous marriage so arresting and dramatic that he used it for Siegfried's parents instead. (And he rejected the name "Signy" for "Sieglinde," the name of Siegfried's mother that appears in the German sources.)

It is Hjordis who preserves the fragments of the sword Gram (Nothung, in Wagner's version) after the death of Siegmund. Thus, Wagner's "Sieglinde" is actually a conflation of Signy and Hjordis.[8] Again, purists may object—but Wagner's decision makes complete dramatic sense and is arguably an improvement on the complex and often confusing storyline of the *Volsunga saga*. Wagner likewise conflated Siegmund with Agnar, a warrior whom Brünnhilde supports in battle contrary to Odin's orders.

One element will disappoint readers coming to this text from Wagner: in the *Volsunga saga* Siegfried is murdered in his bed (and, in this version, Hogni/Hagen is against the plot!). This was obviously far less dramatic and visually interesting than the version in the *Nibelugenlied*, where Siegfried is murdered in the forest. Interestingly, the *Poetic Edda*, in a prose portion, notes that there are conflicting stories about Siegfried's death:

> In this poem the death of Sigurd is related, and here it is said that they killed him outside. But some say this, that they killed him inside, sleeping in his bed. And Germans say that they killed him out in the forest. And the "Old Poem of Gudrun" says that Sigurd and the sons of Giuki were riding to the Assembly when he was killed. But they all say that they treacherously betrayed him when he was lying down and unarmed.[9]

---

[8] Siegmund had a wife between Signy and Hjordis: Borghild, with whom he had two sons.

[9] *Poetic Edda, Brot af Sigurdarkvida*, 176.

Wagner wisely preferred the German version, and so it is this that is portrayed in *Götterdämmerung*.

A couple of other details concerning the *Volsunga saga* may be mentioned here. First, to state the obvious, Wagner "Germanizes" Volsung as "Wälse." In the *Volsunga saga*, Volsung is the great grandson of Odin. However, Wagner actually identifies him with Odin/Wotan, thus eliminating three generations from the clan of the "Wälsungs."

In *Die Walküre*, Siegmund refers to his father (Wälse) as "Wolfe." This is a sly reference to a fascinating portion of the *Volsunga saga*, in which Siegmund and Sinfjotli hide out in the forest, donning wolf skins and changing themselves into wolves for nine days at a time. This tale is told (without the lycanthropy) very briefly by Siegmund in Act One of *Die Walküre*, where it is a recollection of his time with *his* father, Wälse (Wotan). In short, Wagner conflates Siegmund with Sinfjotli.

Consider the genealogy of the Volsung clan . . .

Odin + ?
  ↓
  Sigi + ?
    ↓
    Rerir + ?
      ↓
      Volsung + Ljod
        ↓
        Sigmund & Signy (*twins, and man and wife*)
          ↓
          Sinfjotli

Sigmund + Borghild (*second wife*)
↓
Helgi & Hamund (*sons*)

Sigmund + Hjordis (*third wife*)
↓
 Sigurd + Brynhild
 ↓
 Aslaug

 Sigurd + Gudrun
 ↓
 Sigmund (2) & Svanhild

... in comparison to the Wagnerian genealogy of the Wälsungs:

Wälse [*Volsung plus Wotan/Odin*] + ?
↓
Siegmund [*Sigmund plus Sinfjotli*] & Sieglinde
[*Signy plus Hjordis*] (*twins who marry*)
↓
 Siegfried + Brünnhilde
 (*no issue*)

 Siegfried + Gutrune
 (*no issue*)

To make one last point about the *Volsunga saga*, in it we find Odin continually intervening mysteriously in the story's events, which gave Wagner the idea for Wotan's relatively brief and unexpected appearances in Acts One and Three of *Siegfried*, as well as Sieglinde's recollection, in Act One of *Die Walküre*, of how "the Wanderer" appeared briefly and thrust Nothung into the ash tree (a scene taken directly from the *Volsunga saga*).

As to the lesser sources Wagner utilized, in *Nornagests thattr* Siegfried's foster father is clearly depicted as a dwarf. In *Das Lied vom hürnen Seyfrid*, the Nibelungs and the sons of "King Nibelung" are depicted as dwarfs. One of the sons, "Eugel," is compelled by Siegfried into helping him, utilizing a "cloak of invisibility."

Now let us deal with some loose ends: Wagnerian elements that are difficult to trace to the traditional sources. First of all, Wagnerites are usually shocked to discover that there are no Rhine maidens (or "Rhine daughters," *Rheintöchter*) in Germanic folklore, nor is there any Rhinegold. These seem to be Wagner's invention. However, some mermaids do appear in the *Nibelungenlied* (though not in the Rhine). Depending upon how the text is interpreted, the author may be suggesting that there are three of them—and one is named Sieglinde! (Definitely not to be confused with Siegfried's mother, whom the text also names Sieglinde.) There is nothing in any source about a dwarf trying to woo some mermaids or water nymphs, and there is no "renunciation of love" motif. This is all Wagner's invention.

As to the Rhinegold, in the *Volsunga saga*, Andvari (whom Wagner transforms into Alberich) is living with his gold under a waterfall. (In the *Prose Edda* he lives in a pool of water, and in the *Poetic Edda* he lives under "Andvara-falls"; in all three sources he has taken the form of a fish.) In *Reginsmal* (in the *Poetic Edda*), Loki refers to the gold of Andvari by the kenning "the water's flame." Deryck Cooke speculates that this could have suggested to Wagner the idea of the gold gleaming beneath the surface of the Rhine.[10] Further, Cooke also points out that in all sources except

---

[10] Cooke, 135.

*Thidreks saga* "the Rhine is the treasure's ultimate destination."[11] All of this could have inspired Wagner to create the Rhinegold and the Rhine maidens to guard it. Further, as noted above, Andvari's ring is not a "ring of power." However, the *Nibelungenlied* does very briefly mention a "little rod of gold" amongst the Nibelung treasure which can confer mastery over all humankind.[12] Wagner simply seems to have conflated the ring with the rod.

I have said that Wagner's Alberich is based upon Andvari, but matters are actually more complex than this. Let's start with the name, which actually appears in the *Nibelungenlied*. There we find Siegfried journeying to "Nibelungenland," conquering the kingdom, making vassals of its knights, and seizing the Nibelung treasure. But in doing so he must tangle with a "savage dwarf" named Alberich. Aside from being a dwarf, he has none of the properties with which Wagner endows him and appears only briefly. An "Elberich" also shows up in the fifteenth-century *Heldenbuch*, which Wagner consulted as well. Elberich is "ein wilder Zwerg" (a fierce dwarf), who possesses a ring of invisibility. Only here he is described as "King Elberich the dwarf." It could be, as Cooke conjectures, that both the *Nibelungenlied* and *Heldenbuch* are drawing on some other source in which Alberich/Elberich is the owner of the hoard. In the sixteenth-century *Lied vom hürnen Seyfrid* the hoard belongs to a dwarf named "Nybling." Wagner seems to have consciously synthe-

---

[11] Ibid., 135.

[12] "Nibelung" has various meanings in these sources, and the situation is actually quite confusing. In the *Nibelungenlied* the "Nibelungen" are not dwarfs, and the denotation of the term shifts, eventually referring to the Burgundians.

sized all of this: the dwarf Andvari with his gold becomes Alberich the dwarf and the Nibelung hoard, and the "Nibelungen" become dwarfs. But there is one further component that went into the Alberich of the *Ring*. As noted earlier, in *Thidreks saga* the father of Hagen/Hogni is an "elf." Wagner simply made this a "dark elf" (dwarf) and identified the character with Alberich.

As to Wagner's "Nibelheim," this is his Germanization of the Norse Niflheim. In making this alteration, of course, Wagner connects Niflheim with the Nibelungs. Purists have howled over this, but in fact there is a real etymological connection. Both Old Norse *nifl* and German *Nebel* mean "mist" or "fog" and derive from Proto-Indo-European *\*nebhos*. In compounds, Old Norse *nifl-* suggests darkness. But in all probability "Nibelung" originally meant something like "being of the mist" or possibly "being of darkness." There are no dwarfs in the Norse Niflheim. Instead, they live in Svartalfheim: "dark elf world/home." Though we might have wanted Wagner to distinguish the two, it is not entirely unreasonable to conflate Niflheim and Svartalfheim, and to make Niflheim/Nibelheim the abode of the dark elves given that (1) *nifl-* can carry the connotation of darkness (dark elves, dark place under the earth), and (2) the association of "Nibelung" with dwarfs (Alberich/Elberich and Nybling).

Interestingly, in *Das Lied vom hürnen Seyfrid* the Tarnhelm appears as a *Nebelkap* (mist cap). The term "Tarnhelm" is actually Wagner's coinage. In the *Nibelungenlied* it is a Tarnkappe, only in Middle High German *Kappe* didn't mean a cap, it meant a cape or cloak. However, in the *Nibelungenlied* it only has the power to make the wearer invisible. In Wagner's version alone does it allow one to change shape. Readers may also be surprised to learn that there is no "Tarnhelm" in the Scandinavian sources. Siegfried changes shape with Gunther/Gunnar by using a magic spell (in the *Volsunga saga* it is provided to him by Grimhild, wife of King Giuki). Fans of Fritz Lang's splendid 1924 film *Die Nibelungen* (which deserves a commentary all to itself) will be surprised to hear that in the *Nibelungenlied* Siegfried never changes shape with King Gunther: everything is accomplished entirely by means of the cloak of invisibility. (Lang borrowed the "shape changing" motif from Wagner.)

Finally, we may note that there are numerous references to the runes in *Der Ring des Nibelungen*, where the term has the same variety of meanings it does in the Scandinavian sources. At times it simply seems to mean letters or signs. For example, in Scene Two of *Das Rheingold* Fasolt reminds Wotan of the "runes [*Runen*] of well-considered contract, safeguarded by your spear."[13] At other times, however, *Runen* means magic formulae. For instance, we are told in *Das Rheingold* that "A rune-spell [*Runenzauber*] makes a ring from the gold."[14] In the Prologue of *Götterdämmerung*, Brünnhilde says to Siegfried "I gave to you a bountiful store of hallowed runes [*heiliger Runen*]." And Siegfried says to her "in return for all your runes I hand this ring to you."[15]

This exchange from *Götterdämmerung*, of course, calls to mind the *Sigrdrifumal* in the *Poetic Edda*, and once more demonstrates Wagner's intimate knowledge of the traditional sources. In closing this chapter, I will just remark that a *full* investigation of Wagner's indebtedness to the Germanic tradition—his mythic,

---

[13] Spencer, 74.
[14] Ibid., 82.
[15] Ibid., 285, 286.

philosophic, poetic, and musical sources of inspiration—would be a complete education in the Germanic tradition itself.

## Chapter Four:
# Wotan & the Faustian West

As noted in the Introduction, at the time of the *Ring*'s conception Wagner was an anarchist revolutionary. Major influences on his thinking included Bakunin, Feuerbach, Hegel, and possibly Marx (although of these only Bakunin was an anarchist). Wagner's anarchist ideology is readily apparent not just in his early notes on the *Ring* but in the finished cycle of operas. In the first draft of the *Siegfrieds Tod* libretto (see Chapter One), Siegfried enters Valhalla at the drama's climax, and a sort of anarchist utopia is established on earth. In the 1848 "Sketch" of the *Ring*, Wagner has Brünnhilde cry to the Nibelungs "Not Alberich shall receive [the ring]; no more shall he enslave you, but he himself be free as ye."[1] Here we detect an influence of Hegel's "master-slave dialectic": the master is actually unfree; he only attains true freedom for himself when all are free.

However, as was the case with many anarchists and socialists at the time, Wagner was simultaneously an odd kind of Radical Traditionalist: he believed that the sort of society he wanted to bring about had once existed on earth, in a golden age long gone by, when men lived free of gods and masters, greed and war. Now, we may marvel at the naïveté of this and wish that Wagner had never held this position, but for the moment let us just note that such a tendency, for all its flaws, is quintessentially Western. It is Western both in its intense self-criticism — its radical critique of the present state of Western culture — and in its dream of a

---

[1] Sketch, 311.

perfected, future society.²

However, Wagner did come to shed this naïve anarchism and to radically reconceive the meaning of his own work. And the event that led to this was his encounter with Arthur Schopenhauer's *World as Will and Representation* (published in two volumes in 1818 and 1844). In this work, which is one of the most accessible in all German philosophy, Schopenhauer argues that the world is a manifestation of an infinite, striving force he calls Will. The different species and natural kinds are all "grades of the Will's manifestation." These form a hierarchy, which works out to be more or less identical to the "great chain of being" we find in Aristotle, Schelling, and Hegel. At the top is man, the most perfect objectification of Will. Man is capable of knowing that he is Will—and thus, through man, Will confronts itself.³ This grand vision, however, is profoundly pessimistic. Schopenhauer thought that when mankind confronted itself as Will—or when Will confronted itself (it comes to the same thing)—the result would be horror and a rejection of life. And Schopenhauer urged that on us.

It would be no exaggeration to say that Wagner fell completely under the spell of Schopenhauer's pessimistic vision. He read *The World as Will and Representa-*

---

² For more information see my review of Ricardo Duchesne's *The Uniqueness of Western Civilization* (Leiden-Boston: Brill, 2011) in *North American New Right*, vol. 2, ed. Greg Johnson (San Francisco: Counter-Currents Publishing, 2018). Or better yet, see the book itself.

³ See Arthur Schopenhauer, *The World as Will and Representation*, vol. 1, trans. E. F. J. Payne (Mineola, NY: Dover Publications, 1969), see especially pages 153–54. The Idea that through man Will confronts itself is implicit in Schopenhauer's theory of art.

*tion* four times in its entirety in 1854, during the period of time when he was writing the music of *Die Walküre*. Schopenhauer completely cured Wagner of his revolutionary optimism — and led him to rethink the *Ring*. However, the way that he did so is unusual. Wagner actually changed very little in the libretti of the *Ring* (mainly only tinkering a bit with Brünnhilde's final speech in Act Three of *Götterdammerung*). Instead, he came to realize that the Schopenhauerian perspective was present in the work all along, and that the revolutionary ideology in terms of which he had consciously conceived it was forced and inauthentic.

Wagner wrote the following in a letter to Liszt years later:

> I looked at my poem and saw to my astonishment that what convinced me in Schopenhauer was already there, in my poetic concept. Only then did I really understand my Wotan. I was deeply moved. For years after that, Schopenhauer's book was never far from me. Its ever-growing influence on me and my life was extraordinary and decisive.[4]

In short, for Wagner the *Ring* simply ceased to be a clarion call for a better world, a world without greed and power lust. Instead, it became a reflection on the tragic nature of life, the ineradicability of greed and power lust, and the folly of optimism. And we will see that this is not a case of Wagner simply superimposing a new interpretation on a work already finished. He was, indeed, correct to think that this is the inter-

---

[4] Quoted in M. Owen Lee, *Wagner's Ring: Turning the Sky Around* (New York: Limelight Editions, 1998), 53.

pretation best supported by the work itself.

However, there is much more to the *Ring* than just a pessimistic commentary on life, as I shall discuss. And I will have more to say about Schopenhauer later on, but for now we need to consider another source for Wagner's change of mind, one that usually goes entirely overlooked. Wagnerians normally attribute the shift in Wagner's thinking entirely to his encounter with Schopenhauer. But we must also consider the possibility that Wagner was responding to the peculiar logic of the mythic material he was adapting; that it came to possess him and alter his outlook. Wagner himself gives us plenty of reason to suspect this. Here, in a passage worth quoting at length, is Wagner writing in his autobiography of his encounter with Grimm's *Deutsche Mythologie*:

> All who know the work can understand how the unusual wealth of its contents, gathered from every side, and meant almost exclusively for the student, would react upon me, whose mind was everywhere seeking for something definite and distinct. Formed from the scanty fragments of a perished world, of which scarcely any monuments remained recognizable and intact, I here found a heterogeneous building, which at first glance seemed but a rugged rock clothed in straggling brambles. Nothing was finished, only here and there could the slightest resemblance to an architectonic line be traced, so that I often felt tempted to relinquish the thankless task of trying to build from such materials. And yet I was enchained by a wondrous magic. The baldest legend spoke to me of its ancient home, and soon my whole imagination thrilled with imag-

es; long-lost forms for which I had sought so eagerly shaped themselves ever more and more clearly into realities that lived again. There rose up soon before my mind a whole world of figures, which revealed themselves as so strangely plastic and primitive, that, when I saw them clearly before me and heard their voices in my heart, I could not account for the almost tangible familiarity and assurance of their demeanor. The effect they produced upon the inner state of my soul I can only describe as an entire rebirth. Just as we feel a tender joy over a child's first bright smile of recognition, so now my own eyes flashed with rapture as I saw a world, revealed, as it were, by miracle, in which I had hitherto moved blindly as the babe in its mother's womb.[5]

The mythological material Wagner found in Grimm and the traditional sources touched a chord deep in his Germanic soul and awakened him in new ways. As M. Owen Lee notes, "Like those novelists who tell us that their characters 'take over' the writing and determine their own fates, Wagner acknowledged that his *Ring* was shaping itself from some source beyond his conscious control."[6] And the main character of the *Ring*, of course, is Wotan. Essentially, in writing the *Ring* Wagner came to be possessed by the spirit of Wotan.

He wrote to his friend Röckel, another anarchist:

I started my poem with an optimistic view of the

---

[5] Richard Wagner, *My Life*, trans. Andrew Gray (New York: Da Capo Press, 1992), 260.

[6] Lee, 26.

world . . . and I hardly noticed, when I was outlining it, that I was unconsciously following a quite different and much more profound intuition. I was seeing, not a single moment in the world's evolution [the supersession of capitalism by anarchistic socialism], but the essence of the world, the world in all of its moments.[7]

In Schopenhauer, Wagner found a vocabulary in terms of which he could interpret this "intuition" — but the intuition did not originate with Schopenhauer. It was born of Wagner's study of Germanic myth, and his insight into the "essence of the world" was a product of its spirit.

The myths always say more than any writer makes them say. But Wagner comes closer than anyone to providing the complete mytho-poetic speech for the West. Through his profound engagement with the figure of Wotan, Wagner manages to express the essence of the Western spirit, the spirit of "Faustian man." As I put it another essay:

> Oswald Spengler aptly described the soul of Northern European man as "Faustian." He tells us that the "prime-symbol" of the Faustian is "pure and limitless space": "Far apart as may seem the Christian hymnology of the south and the Eddas of the still heathen north, they are alike in the implicit space-endlessness of prosody, rhythmic syntax and imagery. Read the *Dies Irae* together with the Völuspá, which is little earlier; there is the same adamantine will to overcome and break all resistances of the visi-

---

[7] Quoted in Lee, 53.

ble." The Faustian soul is characterized by a solemn inwardness, tending towards solitude and melancholy—but matched by a ceaseless, outward-striving will. European man has always sought to go beyond: to explore, to find adventures in other lands, to conquer, to peer into the mysterious depths of things, to find new ways to control and manipulate his environment. This is not to say that these qualities are never found in other peoples, but—as Spengler recognized—they are most pronounced and developed in Northern European man.[8]

In telling the story of Wotan, the *Ring* tells the story of the Faustian West. In the same essay I wrote:

We find the Faustian spirit in our gods. Óðhinn is the ceaseless wanderer, and the leader of the wild hunt. From his throne, called Hlidskjalf, he can survey the entire world. His two ravens, Huginn and Muninn (Thought and Memory) fly over the earth, bringing news of all things back to him. But there are secrets concealed even from Óðhinn, and beings (such as the Norns) over which he has no power. Like us, he burns with a desire to know the hidden and to control his fate. So he hung on the windy tree, nights all nine, and won the secret of the runes—the hidden lore that explains all things.

---

[8] See Collin Cleary, *What Is a Rune? & Other Essays* (San Francisco: Counter-Currents Publishing, 2015), 149–50. The quote from Spengler appears in *The Decline of the West*, vol. I, trans. Charles Francis Atkinson (New York: Alfred A. Knopf, 1926), 185–86. See also my review of Ricardo Duchesne's *The Uniqueness of Western Civilization*, op. cit.

He sought wisdom too from Mimir's well (the well of memory) and sacrificed an eye to drink from it. We are Ódhinn, and he is the embodiment of the Faustian spirit.[9]

Wagner wrote to Röckel in 1854: "Observe [Wotan] closely! He resembles *us* to a tee."[10] What Wagner means here is that Wotan represents "modern man" (he goes on to describe Wotan as "the sum total of present-day intelligence" and to contrast him with Siegfried, who is the "man of the future"). But here Wagner falls into the unconscious universalism that is characteristic of Western thinkers: the tendency to project Western features onto humanity as a whole. Obviously, however, Wotan does *not* resemble "modern man" in, for example, the China, India, or Africa of 1854 (or even of today).

In a similarly universalistic vein, Lee writes that "Wotan represents not so much the notion of God as what there is in man that has godlike potential."[11] But this is not fully accurate either. What Wotan represents is the striving of *Western* man for the infinite, for the transcendence of all boundaries—his striving, indeed, to acquire divine wisdom. Wotan represents human consciousness in its Faustian inflection: the restless search for total knowledge, coupled with the

---

[9] Cleary, *What Is a Rune?*, 150.

[10] *Selected Letters of Richard Wagner*, trans. Stewart Spencer and Barry Millington (New York: W.W. Norton, 1988), 308.

[11] Lee, 56–57. In a way, Lee inadvertently hits on a very important point made by Edred Thorsson: that the "Odian" does not worship Odin; instead, he strives to become him. See my essay "What is Odinism?" in *TYR*, vol. 4 (North Augusta, SC: Ultra, 2014).

desire to manipulate and to control all of nature. These are two sides of the same coin. But what Wotan depicts above all else is Faustian, Western man *achieving self-consciousness*: coming to full awareness of his nature—and then willing his own end.

Cooke notes that "it has been mainly Europeans, or men of European origin, who have dominated and despoiled nature on a large scale; and in *The Rhinegold* Wagner was adapting North European myths to present an artistic diagnosis of the ills of *European* civilization."[12] Before we react in knee-jerk fashion against this seemingly "anti-Western" statement of Cooke's, let us just pause to note that *he is right*.

And as a further piece of evidence to support the claim that it is really Western man that is represented in the figure of Wotan, not man in general, let us consider this quote from Wagner's essay *Art and Climate* (1841):

> Yet where climatic nature draws man beneath the all-sheltering influence of her rankest prodigality, and rocks him in her bosom as a mother rocks her child—where we must therefore place the cradle of newborn mankind—there has man remained a child forever—as in the tropics—with all an infant's good and evil qualities. First where she drew this all-conditioning, over-tender influence back, when she handed man, like a prudent mother her adult son, to himself and his own free self-devisings—where man, then, mid the waning warmth of the directly fostering care of climate, was forced to cater for himself—do we see him

---

[12] Cooke, 252. Italics in original.

ripening to the full unfoldment of his being. Only through the force of such a Need as surrounding Nature did not, like an over-careful mother, both listen for and still at once ere it had scarcely risen, but for whose appeasement he must himself provide, did he gain consciousness not only of that need but also of his *power*. This consciousness he reached through learning *the distinction between himself* and from whom he now must *wrest* it, became the object of his observation, inquiry, and dominion.[13]

In short, only an inhospitable climate would have caused man to individuate himself from nature. We do not find this happening, to use Wagner's example, in the Tropics, and so we do not find real history in the Tropics, or art, literature, science, or philosophy on anything other than an extremely rudimentary level. What inhospitable climate does Wagner have in mind, and where, thus, did history begin? He tells us on the next page of the essay:

> Not, therefore, in the teeming Tropics, not in the sensuous flower land of India, was born *true art*; but on the naked, sea-splashed rocks of Hellas, upon the stony soil and beneath the scanty shadows of the olive trees of Attica, was set her cradle:—*for here, amid privations, strove Hercules and suffered*—here was the first *true man* begotten.

And so it is Wagner's view that it is primarily European man who succeeded in separating himself

---

[13] In Ellis, 252.

from nature—and who then turned on nature, so to speak, and sought to dominate her. Thus, if Wotan represents this aspect of "man," it is truly European man that is meant here. Wagner is critical of this Western "will to power," but he also seems to be aware that it is the source of all of our achievements. The early Wagner sought to reform the West, to heal the division Western man had made between himself and nature. The later Wagner saw our nature as inherently *tragic* and offered, as we shall see, a different answer. And of course, Wagner was strongly influenced by Greek drama, in which the tragic nature of (Western) man is central. Oedipus, for example, represents the Western spirit: striving ceaselessly and heedlessly *to know*, until he is destroyed by knowing.

Wotan—Western man—is the tragic character of the *Ring*, and his tragic flaw is his restless, and reckless, pursuit of knowledge and power.

The story of the *Ring* involves four ages, similar to those taught in many traditions. *The Age of Titans* is the period represented by figures somehow more primordial than the gods: Erda, the Norns, the giants, and possibly the Rhine daughters. Events in this age are not depicted in the *Ring*; they are merely referred to (primarily in *Götterdämmerung*). *The Age of Gods* is the time dominated by Wotan and the other divinities (who, aside from Fricka, have little to do in the *Ring*). It is depicted in *Das Rheingold*, and the stage is set for its passing away in *Die Walküre*. *The Age of Heroes* is portrayed in *Siegfried* and the Prologue to *Götterdämmerung*. However, it is really only truly inaugurated in Act Three of *Siegfried*, at the moment when the hero shatters Wotan's spear. Of all the ages, its duration in the *Ring* is the briefest. *The Age of Men*—the decadent "wolf age," equivalent to the Indian Kali Yuga—is depicted in *Götterdämmerung* and really comes into its own when Siegfried is duped into drinking the potion of forgetfulness. The archetypal "men" of this age are Gunther and Hagen. All is lost when Siegfried is murdered, and the age shifts into its final, cataclysmic form: Ragnarok (which Wagner understood to mean *Götterdämmerung*, or "twilight of the gods").[14]

As Lee notes, Wagner wrote to Liszt that the opening music of *Das Rheingold* represented "the beginning of the world."[15] And certainly what the opening scene of that opera depicts is a kind of primordial or original crime: Alberich's theft of the Rhinegold. The Titanic Age is really the time of pre-human, preconscious nature, personified by "the Titans" (to borrow a term, of course, from Greek mythology). These are relatively unconscious beings, almost devoid of personality, who represent the dull, cyclical, pre-determined patterns of the universe that existed for eons prior to the origin of volitional, self-aware human consciousness. For Lee, Alberich's theft represents man's separating himself from—and violating—nature, represented by the Rhinegold and the spirits of nature, the Rhine daughters, who guard it. This is certainly part of Wagner's intention, but Lee overemphasizes it. For it is truly Wotan who represents human—more narrowly Western—consciousness. Wagner's attitude toward this consciousness is critical, but Alberich represents a degraded aspect of it.

In fact, the real "beginning of time" involves Wotan's encounter with the Norns, which is recalled (not depicted) in the Prologue to *Götterdämmerung*. The "First Norn" states:

---

[14] Please note that Wagner never refers to any of these "ages." This is my interpretation.

[15] Lee, 35.

> At the world-ash [Yggdrasil]
> once I wove
> when, tall and strong,
> a forest of sacred branches
> blossomed from its bole;
> in its cooling shade
> there splashed a spring [Mimir's well],
> whispering wisdom,
> its ripples ran:
> I sang then of sacred things. —
>
> A dauntless god
> came to drink at the spring;
> one of his eyes
> he paid as toll for all time:
> from the world-ash
> Wotan broke off a branch;
> the shaft of a spear
> the mighty god cut from its trunk.[16]

With this act, the Age of Titans ends and the Age of the Gods, of Wotan, begins. Represented here is human consciousness arising and separating itself from nature.

Cooke writes, "Before this event, there *were* no events, but only the unconscious world of nature, in which Erda slumbered, the Norns guarded the Well and the Tree, and the Rhinemaidens guarded the Gold; after that event, conscious life began."[17] Indeed, as Cooke has demonstrated in his analysis of Wagner's music, all the *Leitmotive* of the *Ring* are developments of more basic motives, some of which are associ-

---

[16] Spencer, 281.
[17] Cooke, 248.

ated with "unconscious nature" and others with man. But let us allow Wagner to speak for himself. Here is what he writes in the essay *Artwork of the Future*:

> From the moment when man perceived the difference between himself and nature, and thus commenced his own development as *man*, by breaking loose from the unconsciousness of natural animal life — when he thus looked nature in the face and from the first feelings of his dependence on her, thereby aroused, evolved the faculty of thought — from that moment did error begin, as the earliest utterance of consciousness. But error is the mother of knowledge; and the history of the birth of knowledge out of error is the history of the human race, from the myths of primal ages down to the present day.[18]

So, Wotan's drinking from Mimir's well and ripping the branch from the ash tree represents a kind of primordial fall.

And let us now consider what Wotan gives up in order to gain knowledge: he sacrifices an eye, or half his vision. Cooke argues that this represents Wotan's loss of "half of his instinctual being — the half which is the instinct for mutual love and fellowship."[19] And Bryan Magee notes that after the loss of the eye "Never again does [Wotan] see anything straight."[20] In the *Ring*, Wotan is again and again shown to lack insight into himself. He fails to foresee the consequences of

---

[18] Richard Wagner, *The Art-Work of the Future and Other Works*, trans. William Ashton Ellis (Lincoln: University of Nebraska Press, 1993), 70. (Henceforth "Ellis.")

[19] Cooke, 261.

[20] Magee, *The Tristan Chord*, 112.

his actions or to perceive his own true feelings. He has repressed his capacity for love and sought only knowledge and power.

Wotan is blind to love and to the harm he has done to the world. The branch he tears from the world ash tree becomes his spear, symbol of his power. On it he carves runes that express the laws he has decreed and the contracts he has made that bind him and others. (This element in the characterization of Wotan/Odin is largely Wagner's own invention.) But as Wagner notes in his "Sketch," "the peace by which [the gods] have arrived at mastery does not repose on reconcilement: by violence and cunning was it wrought." And then comes this strange statement: "The object [*Absicht*] of their higher ordering of the world is moral consciousness [*sittliches Bewusstsein*]: but the wrong they fight attaches to themselves."[21] This is a tantalizing but obscure comment, almost seeming to suggest a kind of Fichtean conception of Wotan: through his pursuit of mastery, he sought to bring the real into accord with the ideal, but his efforts in that direction were compromised by his own transgressions, his exploitation of nature and of other beings (Freia, the giants, Siegmund, etc.). (This understanding of Wotan is certainly supported by the *Eddas*, in which Odin creates an entirely new world through the transformation of the body of the Titanic Ymir, who dominated the preceding age.)

In all of these doings, Wagner establishes in *Das Rheingold* that Wotan has, in fact, been aided and encouraged by Loge. Just what does Loge represent? Cooke argues that he represents the intellect, and this interpretation certainly seems to be on the right track.

---

[21] Sketch, 302.

Cooke writes that Loge embodies the "elemental power of thought, which, though available to all, will serve only the individual with the determination to harness and use it—and Wotan has harnessed and is using Loge." Cooke writes, further, that intellect (like Loge) is "not always easy to summon, it is difficult to control, often at odds with a man's ideals, instincts, and emotions, and impossible to coerce into producing the answers [the gods] demand."[22]

Loge/Intellect is crafty and cunning, leading Wotan astray and entangling him in making false promises. Cooke refers to Loge as "demonic" and as intellect in its "demonic aspect—as a source of ideas and inspirations."[23] Indeed, the Wotan-Loge relationship bears a strong resemblance to the Faust-Mephistopheles relationship as depicted by Goethe. Cooke does not make this observation, but he does claim that one minor source for the *Ring* was "a popular Faust play" (though he clearly does not mean Goethe's *Faust*, Cooke never says anything else about it[24]). Wagner, of course, was a great reader of Goethe and in 1839 planned a symphony based on *Faust* (only one movement, the *Faust Overture*, survives). And it can be argued there is something "Faustian" about quite a few characters in Wagner, including the Flying Dutchman and Tannhäuser. In Act Two of *Das Rheingold*, Wotan tells Brünnhilde:

> When youthful love's
> delights had faded,

---

[22] Cooke, 169.
[23] Cooke, 173.
[24] Cooke, 131. Cooke died before he could complete his study of the *Ring*, and only the first volume was ever published.

> I longed in my heart for power:
> impelled by the rage
> of impulsive desires,
> I won for myself the world.
> Unwittingly false
> I acted unfairly,
> binding by treaties
> what boded ill:
> cunningly Loge led me on
> but vanished while roaming the world.[25]

Here we cannot help but be reminded of Mephistopheles egging Faust on in his restless search for satisfaction.

And just as Mephistopheles does with Faust, Loge also manages to confront Wotan with certain truths. Indeed, he is one of the agents of Wotan's increasing self-awareness throughout the *Ring* (in addition to Fricka, Brünnhilde, Erda, and others). In *Das Rheingold*, Loge effectively confronts Wotan with the fact that he cannot both dominate the world and seek love. He also speaks about love as the great creative element in life — something Wotan will not recognize until much later in the *Ring*.

Loge's character suggests the dual nature of intellect: it has the potential both to reveal truth and to manipulate and distort. It is almost irresistible to see *logos* in "Loge" (though, of course, there is no real etymological relation). There is also a close kinship, however, between Loge and the Greek conception of *technē*. As noted earlier, Wagner makes Loge the god of fire, and if Cooke is right about Loge representing intellect, it is surely the promethean fire that is meant

---

[25] Spencer, 149.

here. Loge says the following to Alberich in Scene Three of *Das Rheingold*:

> You know me well,
> you childish elf?
> Then say who I am
> that you yelp like that.
> In a frozen hole,
> where you coweringly lay,
> who'd have given you light
> and warming fire
> if Loge hadn't smiled upon you?
> What use would your forgework
> have been
> if I hadn't heated your forge?
> I am your kinsman
> and once was your friend:
> so your thanks seem far from fitting![26]

As Cooke puts it, Loge helps the dwarfs "with their technical labour."[27] And we may also note that Wagner uses the same musical motive to represent both Loge's craftiness (as displayed in *Das Rheingold*) and the "magic fire" that appears in *Die Walküre* and *Götterdämmerung*.

Though Loge is never seen again (in anthropomorphic form) after *Das Rheingold*, he does appear twice more, in his elemental form, as fire. First, Loge appears in *Die Walküre*, just after Wotan has the inspiration to draw together Siegfried with Brünnhilde, by surrounding her with a ring of fire only the hero can penetrate. (Cooke points out, correctly, that this is ac-

---

[26] Spencer, 95.
[27] Cooke, 210.

tually Brünnhilde's idea, though here she is surely speaking once more as Wotan's will.) Second, and most significantly, Loge appears as the cataclysmic fire that destroys Walhalla and the world at the climax of *Götterdämmerung*.

In light of the foregoing remarks on the nature of Loge, it is irresistible to conclude that at the end of the *Ring, intellect consumes all.* The *Ring* is really the story of Wotan's attainment of self-awareness, as an indirect result of his almost entirely "extroverted" search for knowledge and power. In this, as I have noted, he is aided by several figures who confront him with the truth about himself and who act as extensions or personifications of his being (including Loge and Brünnhilde). In the end, Wotan's "intellect," his quest for knowledge, comes full circle: he achieves consciousness of himself and, in true Schopenhauerian fashion, wills "the end" (*das Ende*), through the agent of his will, Brünnhilde, who uses Loge/fire/intellect to engulf the world in flames.

But it is imperative that we always bear in mind the fact that Wotan is the symbol of Western man. If we read the whole story of Wotan's quest and its fiery climax with this in mind, it is impossible not to think of the present predicament of modern, Western man. Like Wotan, he has sought limitless knowledge and power. He has conquered almost the entire earth and most of its peoples, then sailed off to the stars in search of more. At all times he has been moved both by a desire for adventure and by ideals of aesthetic and moral perfection. But now, just when Western man has reached the height of scientific and technological achievement, when he has finally created a world of plenty largely free of hardship and disease, like Faust he feels satisfied and has seemingly lost the will to go on. Worse yet, he has damned himself according to ideals that were, in fact, his own creation—and, like Wotan, he has willed his own death and displacement.

Inspired by the Germanic mythological material, Wagner has done much more than offer a commentary on modernity (as he had originally envisioned). The *Ring*, in fact is a work of prophecy: Wagner gives us Western man's past, present, and—so it would seem—future. But does the *Ring* offer us, in the end, nothing more than a tragic picture of the West, culminating in its self-immolation? I believe that it does offer us more, but to see this we must delve deeper. There is still much more to be said about the *Ring*. Let's consider Wotan's character in greater detail, taking each of the four operas in turn.

# CHAPTER FIVE:
## *DAS RHEINGOLD*

When the events of *Das Rheingold* begin, the Wotan-Loge relationship is already well-established, and the primeval crimes described earlier are long past. However, the opera opens with yet another crime against nature: Alberich's theft of the Rhinegold. This opening scene is tied to the very end of the *Ring*: the conflagration set in motion by Brünnhilde expiates the "original sin" of Alberich's theft (and of Wotan's actions), and Wagner links the two scenes musically. As I shall discuss more fully later on, we are thus left with the sense of a return to the beginning, of cycles continuing without end.

But let us now consider just who Alberich is. He represents, in fact, the darker aspect of man's emergence from nature and quest to control her. Alberich seeks wealth and crude, lawless power. Further, he is motivated in large measure by envy and resentment. He envies the power, carefree lives, and beauty of the gods. And he resents the Rhine daughters for their rejection of him. He is an ugly, misshapen, unwanted creature. And when he renounces love, it is really life that he is renouncing. Alberich sets himself against life, and seeks to despoil and degrade all that is better than he. (It is clear that Wagner taught Nietzsche a thing or two about *ressentiment*.) Whereas Wotan (in a good mood) seeks to transform otherness according to his ideals, Alberich seeks essentially to annihilate it.

In *The Artwork of the Future*, Wagner writes of the "absolute egoist," who is surely represented by Alberich: "The terrible thing about the absolute egoist is that he sees in other human beings nothing but the natural means of his own existence, and — even if in a quite particular, barbaric-cultivated way — *consumes* them, like the fruits and animals of nature, and thus will not *give*, but only *take*."[1] But why must Alberich renounce love in order to acquire the power of the ring? Cooke argues that it is because wielding that power will require slave labor, and so he who would have it must renounce love for humanity. But surely what is also involved is the renunciation of love of nature itself — of existence, really. The attitude of love, whether it is love for one person, or for humanity, or for nature, involves a kind of openness to what is other. But the power sought by Alberich entails a total aggrandizement of the self and a closing off to otherness.[2] This "closing off" takes the form of destroying or corrupting what is other. It is obvious, however, that the standpoint of Wotan has the potential to shade off into that of Alberich, seeking to manipulate or destroy all that which does not conform to one's ideals. And so in *Die Walküre* we do indeed find Wotan confessing that he has come to be tempted by the "dark side."

In addition to this psychological (or metaphysical) dynamic, there is, of course, a political dimension to what Wagner is saying. And there is a theory of history here as well. For Wagner, the rise of Alberich represents a shift in modern power relations. In historical terms, Wotan represents rule by the aristocracy, who,

---

[1] Quoted in Cooke, 261.

[2] Alberich represents what I termed "Will" in my essay "Knowing the Gods" (note that my use of "Will" is not to be confused with Schopenhauer's). See Collin Cleary, *Summoning the Gods* (San Francisco: Counter-Currents Publishing, 2011).

once upon a time, were men of adventure, daring, and curiosity. This was rule by the noble, according to laws, contracts, and a code of honor. Alberich, on the other hand, represents the rise of the capitalist middle class, who were moved in no small measure by resentment against the aristocracy and a lust for the external trappings of aristocratic life, without the underlying honor and nobility they served to signify. While the rule of the aristocracy might have been, at times, despotic, the middle class sought to put in its place an even more debased system, one ruled entirely by greed and largely devoid of any conception of *noblesse oblige*.

George Bernard Shaw, in his classic essay on Wagner's *Ring*, describes Alberich quite well: "It is just as if some poor, rough, vulgar, coarse fellow were to offer to take part in aristocratic society, and be snubbed into the knowledge that only as a millionaire could he ever hope to bring that society to his feet and buy himself a beautiful and refined wife. His choice is forced on him."[3] Anarchist-socialist though he may have been, it is quite clear that Wagner is much more sympathetic to the aristocracy than he is to the middle class. In *The Artwork of the Future*, he blames the decline of art on its passing from the control of the aristocracy to that of the middle class philistine, "the most heartless and cowardly creation of our civilization."[4]

Repeatedly in the *Ring*'s libretto, Wagner describes Alberich as motivated by envy. And it is clear that wealth is merely a means to power for Alberich—a

---

[3] G.B. Shaw, *The Perfect Wagnerite* (New York: Time Incorporated, 1972), 3. (Originally published 1898.)

[4] Quoted in George S. Williamson, *The Longing for Myth in Germany* (Chicago: University of Chicago Press, 2004), 202.

means, really, to exact his revenge upon life. When Wotan and Loge encounter Alberich in Nibelheim, the dwarf berates the two gods: "You who live, laugh and love up there in the breath of gentle breezes: in my golden grasp I'll capture all you gods! As love has been forsworn by me, so all that lives shall also forswear it: lured by gold, you'll lust after gold alone!"[5] Basically, he sees the gods as time-wasting, life-loving aristocrats. His is the voice of middle-class greed and "practicality."

Of course, if we return to my claim that Wotan specifically represents Western man, then Alberich takes on a whole new significance. (As does Wagner's contrast, which I shall come to in a moment, between "Light Alberich" and "Dark Alberich.") In this case, Wotan clearly represents European man conceived as *árya*, as noble: he dwells in the hyperborean regions, pursues knowledge, is "dauntless" and *thumotic*, is concerned with honor and the rule of law, etc. By contrast, Alberich, Mime, and the Nibelung minions are dark, squat, consumed by envy and greed, dishonorable, and conniving. Understood in "racialist" terms (and critics of Wagner often read him this way), the threat posed by Alberich represents not just the ascendency of the middle class, but the "rising tide of color."

Reading Alberich either with this interpretation in mind, or the more conventional one concerning the rise of the middle class, it is important to note that it is Wotan himself who paves the way for Alberich. Over time, Wotan's rule loses its legitimacy as he connives and cheats and makes false promises. Wotan's rule is also inherently harmful—and is so from the very be-

---

[5] Spencer, 96.

ginning, when he rips the branch from the ash tree, thereby setting in motion the death of the natural world itself. The stifling character of his laws is embodied by Fricka, who uses them to force Wotan into destroying his beloved Siegmund as revenge against Siegmund's "transgression" with Sieglinde. (And as Cooke points out, Fricka is "symbolically barren," because Wotan's laws are barren.[6])

The response to Wotan's rule comes in two waves. First there is Alberich, who seeks power through wealth, not through daring or through knowledge. And after him comes Siegfried, the innocent who would wipe away the old order. Although Wagner clearly sympathizes with Wotan, he viewed the desire for power *as such* to be inimical to life. Therefore, he treats Wotan and Alberich as two expressions of the same principle. Wagner has Wotan refer to himself as "Light Alberich" and to Alberich as "Dark Alberich." Alberich is just a darker, perverted version of the desire for power—though Wagner believed that even the "light" version is inherently pernicious. One can therefore see that at the heart of Nietzsche's rebellion against Wagner was his belief that the "will to power," as exhibited by Wotan, could be noble. For Nietzsche, Wagner fails to see that Alberich's power lust is something qualitatively different: the twisted, hate-filled power lust of the misshapen slave type.

Cooke makes a number of perceptive comparisons between Wotan and Alberich.[7] Both are out to gain power by exploiting nature, and both encounter (and despoil) nature while it is under the guard of three "wise-women" (the Norns, the Rhine daughters). The

---

[6] Cooke, 152.
[7] See Cooke, 148–49.

contrasts, of course, are just as interesting. Whereas Wotan originally sought knowledge, Alberich sought only power. The former's quest is satisfied, whereas the latter's is not. Alberich gave up love in order to attain power; Wotan gave up an eye to gain the knowledge that would lead to power. And as Cooke puts it, this left him "blind to the claims of love."[8] However, Wotan's power was bound by his laws, whereas Alberich seeks unconditional power, motivated by envy and a desire for revenge.

Over time, however, Wotan becomes more like Alberich, tiring of love and seeking power for its own sake. He tells Brünnhilde in Act Two of *Die Walküre*, "When youthful love's delights had faded, I longed in my heart for power."[9] Wotan's willingness in *Das Rheingold* to risk the loss of the beautiful Freia is indicative of his loss of interest in love. And once he has attained the ring from Alberich he is almost seduced by it: "Now I hold that which exalts me, the mightiest lord of the mighty!" And later (to Fafner): "Brazenly ask for whatever you want, everything will I grant you; but not for the world shall I give up the ring!"[10] When Erda appears and counsels Wotan to give up the ring, she does *not* warn that its possession will literally bring about the end of the gods. In effect, she advises him not to allow the ring to corrupt him in this, the final phase of his existence.

In the end, although Wotan clearly envies the unbridled power the ring confers on Alberich, he cannot follow the dwarf and give up love entirely. His love for Brünnhilde, in fact, is what paves the way for her union with Siegfried (when he accedes to her wish to

---

[8] Cooke, 159.
[9] Spencer, 149.
[10] Spencer, 105, 111.

be surrounded by the ring of fire). And this in turn leads to the loss of his own power. In his final hours — as Waltraute informs us — Wotan pines for Brünnhilde, as his army of the dead heaps the remains of the world ash around Walhalla to prepare for his own immolation. In the end, Wotan regains his sight and allows love to triumph over power.

## Chapter Six:
# *Die Walküre*

Wotan schemes to win back the ring, siring the race of the Wälsungs. His plan is that Siegmund will be a "free hero" unbound by any of the agreements Wotan has made. In his "Sketch" Wagner also refers to Siegmund as a "free will" — implying that Wotan is fundamentally unfree. The truth is that the god is not all powerful. Wotan rules only by means of the agreements and the laws he has made, which he is honor-bound to uphold. But Wotan's plot yet again reveals his blindness. There are forces at work in the coming of the Wälsungs that Wotan himself does not control.

For example, why does Wotan beget twins? He only needs Siegmund, after all. And yet Sieglinde is produced as well. These two are fated to meet in adulthood and produce Siegfried. But Wotan does not know this, and he is not the one who has fated it to be. Not only does Wotan lack omniscience, he is physically vulnerable as well. Siegmund's description of life with his father "Wolfe" indicates this: "Outlawed, the old man fled with me, deep in the wildwood."[1] Wotan is not fully in control of the situation and does not entirely foresee the consequences of his actions. In fact, his scheme to gain the ring actually leads to the end of the gods, who cannot be saved.

In *Die Walküre* Wotan comes to realize his own lack of consciousness. The first to help him confront himself is Fricka, who forces Wotan to recognize that Siegmund is not a "free will" at all: Wotan has manipulated him every step of the way. But the most signifi-

---
[1] Spencer, 127.

cant agent of Wotan's self-understanding is Brünnhilde. She is, of course, Wotan's child with Erda, who had counselled him at the conclusion of *Das Rheingold* and from whom he had ardently sought to learn more. In Act Three of *Siegfried*, Erda will tell Wotan "You are not what you say you are!"[2] But it is chiefly through Brünnhilde that Erda instructs Wotan; she is a means by which he can attain true knowledge—not of the world, but of himself. Again and again it is women who reveal Wotan to himself.

He speaks the following to Brünnhilde: "To my loathing I find only ever myself in all that I encompass! That other self for which I yearn, that other self I never see; for the free man has to fashion himself— serfs are all I can shape!"[3] When Wotan utters these words in *Die Walküre*, he does not yet know that that free man will be Siegfried, who will fashion himself as he does the sword Nothung. And he does not know that Siegfried—together with Brünnhilde—will bring about his own destruction. Yet Wotan yearns for this, telling Brünnhilde in the same conversation, "Let all I raised now fall in ruins! My work I abandon; one thing alone do I want: the end—the end."[4]

Recall that Wotan also confessed to Brünnhilde that he had begun to lose interest in love and to yearn instead for power. However, it is Brünnhilde who reawakens Wotan's capacity for love. When she disobeys Wotan, acting out of love for Siegmund, she forces Wotan to confront his own love for the hero and to understand that she acted according to his own heart's true desire. As Cooke points out, it is only through Siegmund's love for Sieglinde—so movingly ex-

---

[2] Spencer, 257.
[3] Spencer, 152.
[4] Spencer, 153.

pressed in his refusal to enter Walhalla without her—that Siegmund becomes truly independent of Wotan.[5] In both Brünnhilde and Siegmund, therefore, it is love that threatens Wotan's carefully-laid plans. Of course, Wotan is also moved by his love for Brünnhilde and grants her request to be encircled by a fire that only the greatest of all heroes can pass through. Here Wotan sets the stage for the triumph of love itself: the union of Brünnhilde and Siegfried.

"Love" was, indeed, the original "message" of the *Ring* and Wagner's solution to our modern problems. When I first heard that "love is the answer," I was terribly disappointed, and for a long time I thought there was nothing in Wagner for me except the music. I believe this is one of the reasons so many who are interested in the Germanic tradition have shied away from Wagner and seen him as a distorter. As I will argue shortly, however, there's much more to Wagner's "love" than meets the eye, and it is not quite as "mushy" as one would think. And, of course, it must be reiterated that Wagner abandoned this "love is the answer" message—though love is still held up in the *Ring* as a kind of supreme ideal.

---

[5] Cooke, 306.

## Chapter Seven:
# *Siegfried*

If Wotan is the main character of the *Ring*, Siegfried is its hero. However, in dealing with the character of Siegfried we do not depart from our discussion of Wotan at all. This is because Siegfried, like many of the other characters in the *Ring*, is a kind of hypostatization of an aspect of Wotan himself. We have already seen this in several cases. Loge represents the crafty, creative-destructive intellect utilized by Wotan, which eventually leads him astray. Fricka is the personification of Wotan's rigid and barren laws. Brünnhilde is the embodiment of Wotan's will. Alberich is Wotan's dark side, which he finds himself inclining toward, as he confesses in *Die Walküre*. What, then, does Siegfried represent?

Let us consider once more Wotan's words to Brünnhilde: "To my loathing I find only ever myself in all that I encompass! That other self for which I yearn, that other self I never see; for the free man has to fashion himself — serfs are all I can shape!"[1] Siegfried is a counterpart self to Wotan. Of course, the same could be said of Alberich, but here the relationship is of an entirely different order. While Alberich represents Wotan's dark alter ego, which he abhors, Siegfried represents an ideal that Wotan longs for. In a certain sense, Siegfried possesses something Wotan lacks. Just what is this? The most obvious answer is *freedom* — Wotan makes this clear in the lines just quoted. Siegfried is free of the entanglements that restrict Wotan. But there is something else at work here as well.

---

[1] Spencer, 152.

In Act Three of *Siegfried*, when the god and hero confront one another, Siegfried comments on Wotan's missing eye. Wotan responds:

Mit dem Auge,
das als and'res mir fehlt,
erblick'st du selber das eine,
das mir zum Sehen verblieb.

Rendering this into English is somewhat tricky. Spencer, the most reliable English interpreter of the *Ring* libretti, gives us the following somewhat inventive, but thought-provoking translation:

With the eye which,
as my second self, is missing,
you yourself can glimpse the one
that's left for me to see with.[2]

Other translations don't quite know what to do with *das als and're*, and just leave it out. (The translation included with one CD release of *Siegfried* gives the lines as follows: "With the very eye that's missing in me you yourself are looking at the one I still see with.")

Obviously, we are being told that Siegfried possesses Wotan's missing eye, at least in the sense that he possesses some form of perception that Wotan lacks. Of course, we know that Wotan's powers of perception are deficient in at least a couple of different ways. First, gripped by his lust for power and hemmed in by his own laws, Wotan has grown largely insensitive to natural sentiments, especially love. Sec-

---

[2] Spencer, 262.

ond, he lacks self-understanding. When the god and hero clash, note what Wotan says his missing eye is doing, as it sits in Siegfried's skull. *It is looking at Wotan.* It therefore seems reasonable to surmise that Wotan is referring to his own lack of self-awareness, and perhaps indicating that, unlike him, Siegfried truly possesses this virtue: Siegfried, in other words, stands at a higher level of consciousness.

This interpretation is certainly well supported by the remarks Wagner makes about Siegfried in his "Sketch" for the *Ring*. There, Siegfried is portrayed as an innocent, free even of knowledge of the gods. At the same time, however, he is portrayed as a fully conscious, self-actualized being. When Wagner writes of Wotan's (or, in the "Sketch," "the gods'") plan to sire the race of the Wälsungs, he states that "In man they therefore seek to plant their own divinity, to raise his strength so high that, *in full knowledge of that strength*, he may rid him of the gods' protection, to do of his free will what his own mind inspires."[3] A page later Wagner states that in the "rightful hero" (Siegfried) "his self-reliant strength shall reach full consciousness." Later in the "Sketch" he has Siegfried say, "Show me the chance of mastering the gods, and I must work my main to vanquish them."[4]

And yet in the finished *Ring*, Siegfried comes off as anything but fully-conscious. He is indeed a total innocent, but he seems lacking in introspection or self-awareness. And, of course, he is duped in *Götterdämmerung* into an even deeper state of unconsciousness. That this, in fact, came to be Wagner's own understanding of the character is confirmed by two passages

---

[3] Sketch, 302–303, emphasis added.
[4] Sketch, 308.

from Cosima Wagner's diaries, summarizing conversations with Wagner. The first is from July 2, 1872: "Which is the greater, Wotan or Siegfried? Wotan the more tragic, since he recognizes the guilt of existence and is atoning for the error of creation." And consider especially the entry from July 4, 1873: "after lunch conversation about Siegfried and Brünnhilde, the former not a tragic figure, since he does not become conscious of his position."[5]

It therefore seems likely that Cooke is closer to the mark when he interprets the "missing eye" motif as follows: "Siegfried, Wagner's projection of 'natural man,' inspired at this moment [in Act Three] entirely by his instinctive need for mutual love and fellowship (which he will soon find in Brünnhilde), has the eye (symbolizing that instinctive need) that Wotan lacks."[6] In other words, Siegfried does not represent greater self-consciousness. Instead, he actually represents a kind of *unselfconscious naturalness*. This treatment of the character, by the way, is entirely in keeping with how he is portrayed in the *Nibelungenlied* and other sources, in which he comes close to being a sort of heroic dolt.

Now, this interpretation may seem odd. Shouldn't Wotan's ideal "other self" possess the self-consciousness he lacks? Not necessarily. Wotan is flawed in that he lacks self-consciousness, and only gradually comes to attain it. But his deeper flaw — from Wagner's perspective — is the divorce between his intellect and his natural sentiments. It is his unquenchable thirst for knowledge and control that leads to the death of nature itself, as represented by the ash tree. His attain-

---

[5] Quoted in Spencer, 371, note 157.
[6] Cooke, 262.

ment of self-awareness is a good thing *only* in that it reveals to him the harm he has done. Of course, it also leads him to will his own end, and an end to the world itself. Wotan's great sin, therefore, is not fundamentally his lack of self-awareness *as such*, but his lack of awareness specifically of the way in which he has allowed his intellect to shut him off from the natural world, and natural feelings.

The transition from the Age of Gods to the Age of Heroes in the *Ring* is therefore really the transition from a kind of "head-centered," emotionally retarded, overly "intellectual" approach to life, to one that is innocent, natural, unselfconscious, and centered in the heart. When the "head-centered" orientation comes to full consciousness of itself, it is horrified by its barrenness and by the destruction it has caused, and it wills its own end. It yearns for the state of "no mind" — thus opening the door to the "heart-centered" orientation, which knows without knowing and acts without acting.

Once again, it is hard for us Westerners not to identify with Wotan. Like him, we have also lived a head-centered existence, seeking to manipulate and control everything through knowledge. And the result has been disconnection from nature and from our own natural sentiments — in myriad ways. Because Westerners are highly self-critical, we long ago realized this, or the best of us did. And we experienced a kind of self-loathing, which often manifests itself in a yearning for a simpler, pre-modern existence, and in an idealization of "non-Western cultures." This self-loathing is oddly characteristic of the West. There is a perennial idea that nags at us: perhaps life would be better if we knew less and felt more. Hence the Rousseauian idealization of the "noble savage." There is quite a generous dollop or two of this in the *Ring*, and in general what we find in Wagner is an expression of this perennial Western uneasiness about our Faustian nature and longing for the peace of the primitive and unselfconscious life.

Siegfried is like Nietzsche's "child": he is "innocence and forgetting, a new beginning, a game, a self-propelled wheel, a first movement, a sacred 'Yes.'"[7] He has thrown off all the old sins, laws, "hang-ups," and "head games" of the "older generation." He is the new Western man, free of all the baggage of the past. And he is, of course, the revolutionary ideal. When Siegfried kills the dragon Fafner he is striking at the very heart of greed and power lust.[8] He gains the creature's gold as a consequence, but of course the gold comes with a curse! Wagner seems to be saying that there is no "clean" way to have wealth, that it always corrupts.

With the disappearance of Wotan from the scene, we enter very briefly into what can be described in the *Ring*'s cycle of time as the "revolutionary phase" (i.e., the Age of Heroes). The idea here is that Siegfried and Brünnhilde will create together a world free of inhuman laws, hierarchy, greed, power lust, and oppression—a world ruled by love alone. The usual dream, in other words. But all this is merely suggested, never depicted in the *Ring*. Here Wagner is true to his anarchist roots: like all anarchists he is completely and totally vague when it comes to communicating what the

---

[7] Friedrich Nietzsche, *Thus Spoke Zarathustra*, trans. Walter Kaufmann (New York: Penguin Books, 1986), 27.

[8] The esoteric meaning of dragon slaying is the killing of the undeveloped ego and its tendency to "hang on," or to grasp senselessly at things it would be well rid of—like the dragon who hoards a treasure it cannot possibly use.

promised future utopia will actually look like.

Let us now briefly consider just what Wagner meant by "love." As I suggested earlier, one feels a rather strong urge to dismiss this as gooey, high-minded claptrap—but we need to resist that. Cooke writes that "the love that Wagner envisaged is by no means one of the kinds of love so dear to the romantics as a nostrum—idealized sexual love or a feeling of affectionate benevolence; it is an active *social* force, at once sexual, compassionate, self-sacrificial, and creative."[9] But what can this mean? Here we may get some help from Feuerbach, who wrote "Love is the universal law of intelligence and nature—it is nothing else than the realization of the unity of the species through the medium of moral sentiment."[10] In other words, love is "fellow feeling," a sense of identification with another person.[11]

But how is love the answer to greed and power lust, and specifically to modern capitalism, which was clearly one of Wagner's targets? The problem with capitalism, quite simply, is that it sets members of a nation against one another through class warfare. Under the ethos of capitalism, individuals are driven to benefit themselves (and, at most, their immediate families) even if this involves the exploitation of others and the adoption of practices that may harm the larger society in the long run.[12] The radical socialist cure for

---

[9] Cooke, 275. Italics in original.

[10] Ludwig Feuerbach, *The Essence of Christianity*, trans. George Eliot (New York: Harper and Row, 1957), 266.

[11] Though it is also possible to have such feelings for nature as a whole, for animals, and, some people claim, for God—though I don't know what this means, unless God is here understood as the personification of nature.

[12] In Wagner's view aristocracy is less pernicious,

this, of course, is to eradicate the distinction between bosses and workers, haves and have-nots. But no amount of wealth redistribution can make a nation whole, unless one can foster in the people genuine fellow-feeling — in other words, love of one's own.

If this could be effected, and if suitable social and economic reforms were adopted, it might not even be necessary to eliminate the market economy. There would still be bosses and workers, but they would be united in something higher than economic relations: they would have the sense of belonging together in one nation, which would promote social-spiritedness, generosity, and cooperation between all men, regardless of their "class." This was essentially the vision promoted by Hegel in his *Philosophy of Right*. And it was essentially what Fascism and National Socialism promised. (If Hitler was not inspired in his socio-economic views by Wagner, he at least found those views confirmed and reinforced by him.) Also, I cannot resist pointing out that "love" as an answer to capitalism is the message of another great work of art, Fritz Lang's *Metropolis*.[13]

Did Wagner see the social role of love in such "nationalistic" terms? In Chapter One, I noted that Wagner was a German nationalist—but at the same time a kind of internationalist as well. (And I noted, further, that this was not an unusual combination for German nationalists.) We can be fairly certain that Wagner hoped that the love that could unite a nation could also transcend national boundaries and create a "fami-

---

though it involves rigid class distinctions, and at its very worst tends toward a hard-hearted, "let them eat cake" attitude about the less fortunate.

[13] *Metropolis* was co-written by Lang's wife Thea von Harbou, who later became a National Socialist.

ly of man." Of course, in the process of writing the *Ring*, Wagner came to see that although love was still the highest ideal, it was not the final answer. As we shall see, love has the potential to effect great change, but ultimately it never completely triumphs over wickedness.

## Chapter Eight:
# GÖTTERDÄMMERUNG

*Götterdämmerung* takes place in the final, decadent age: the Age of Men, the *Kali Yuga*. Siegfried and Brünnhilde are a bit like two love-struck hippies who have succeeded in toppling The System—and managed to inherit its wealth. But, of course, it is cursed. And in a world where "love" supposedly reigns, and greed and power lust are out of style, there are still human envy and vanity to contend with. This is, in fact, what ultimately destroys the love of Siegfried and Brünnhilde and hastens the world to its end. The Age of Men could also be accurately described as an age of envy.

King Gunther needs to take a bride, but why does he set his sights on Brünnhilde? Why not a nice girl who's not surrounded by a ring of fire and didn't used to be a fierce Valkyrie? The answer is that he wants the prestige of winning Brünnhilde, since everybody knows she can only be won by a hero. Of course, Gunther is incapable of doing the job himself, so he recruits Siegfried to do it for him, while keeping it a secret from others so that he can enjoy all the unearned admiration. The psychology here is nothing new, but it is difficult to fathom (unless one happens to be a self-aware Gunther-type, which is rare). How could anyone enjoy receiving the admiration of others, if he knows it is all based on a lie?

Gunther is not alone here; his sister Gutrune is cut from the same cloth, though this is less obvious. When Hagen floats the idea of Gutrune marrying Siegfried she responds, "You mock me, wicked Hagen! How should I ever bind Siegfried? If he's the world's most glorious hero, the loveliest women on earth would have wooed him long ago."[1] These words reveal Gutrune's insecurity. Though she is a princess of Burgundy, she obviously does not think she has the qualities necessary to win Siegfried's love. And does she perhaps also feel a frisson of excitement at the thought of having a man wanted by so many other women? When Hagen proposes that she give Siegfried the magic potion, making him love her and forget all other women, Gutrune agrees without any hesitation whatsoever — even though she must realize that the hero's "love" will be completely artificial, and her "winning" of him a cheat.

In the persons of Gunther and Gutrune we encounter a human trait not depicted so far in the *Ring*: the desire for unearned prestige. Rousseau, with whose works Wagner was familiar, discusses this as one of the traits that emerges when men band together in civilized society. He remarks that the "rank and fate" of each man is dependent upon natural qualities such as intellect, beauty, strength, and talent: "And since these qualities were the only ones that could attract consideration, he was soon forced to have them or to affect them. It was necessary, for his advantage, to show himself to be something other than what he in fact was." And near the end of the same text he remarks that "the savage lives in himself; the man accustomed to the ways of society is always outside himself and knows how to live only in the opinion of others."[2] Rousseau's is the original description of the "culture

---

[1] Spencer, 291.
[2] From *The Discourse on the Origin of Inequality*, in *Jean-Jacques Rousseau: Basic Political Writings*, trans. Donald A. Cress (Indianapolis: Hackett Publishing, 1987), 67, 81.

of narcissism." Most people are content to "fake it" and will do almost anything to gain or to preserve esteem in the eyes of their fellows. They will even destroy the highest ideal, as Gunther is willing to destroy Siegfried in order to preserve his secret.

In contrast to Gunther and Gutrune, Hagen is motivated by greed and power lust. In Hagen, child of Alberich, these old ills rear their ugly heads once more; they simply will not go away. Love cannot vanquish them for the simple reason that some people do not have the capacity to love, as appears to be the case with Hagen.[3] When love is directed at them, they smell weakness—and use the lover's love to their own advantage. And love fails as well because some people simply aren't lovable. Hagen uses the vanity of Gunther and Gutrune to further his own ends: acquiring the ring of power and killing Siegfried. He places them in a situation where the death of Siegfried becomes necessary, mainly in order to preserve Gunther's "honor" (since Brünnhilde claims publicly that Siegfried has lain with her—and since Siegfried could divulge Gunther's secret). Of course, Hagen himself is really the pawn of his father, Alberich.

The vanity and narcissism of Gunther and Gutrune are just as completely opposed to love as are the power lust of Wotan and the greed of Alberich. And this is no accident, for all these phenomena are manifestations of what Plato called "*thumos.*" *Thumos* is the part of the soul that is neither appetitive nor rational but instead seeks honor and prestige. It can respond with violence when honor is challenged or besmirched.[4]

---

[3] The inheritance of acquired characteristics: Alberich, Hagen's father, renounces love; Hagen is born without it.

[4] See my review essay of Ricardo Duchesne's *The Uniqueness of Western Civilization*, op. cit.

There are higher and lower forms of *thumos* in the *Ring*, and the highest is depicted in Wotan. His thirst for knowledge and mastery is *thumotic* in character. The only other semi-positive portrayal of *thumos* in the *Ring* is Siegfried's heroic bellicosity.

All the other forms of *thumos* in the drama are, by comparison, degenerate. None is worse than that of Alberich, who seeks—out of pure envy and nihilism—to compel others to recognize him or be destroyed. His brother, Mime, is essentially moved by the same desire. And one sees, of course, that Hagen is his father's son. As I have argued, Gunther and Gutrune also seek recognition, brought about this time not through force but through fakery. Even Fricka exhibits a *thumotic* side: her insistence that Wotan punish Siegmund is motivated largely by the fact that, as goddess of home and marriage, she takes his love for Sieglinde as an affront against her authority and her honor.

Thus, one could argue that the major conflict in the *Ring* is really between *thumos* and *agape*.[5] In other words, the conflict is between two sorts of "other-directed" impulse: one that seeks to raise the self above the other in some fashion (through thoroughly knowing it, controlling it, or compelling its recognition), and one that seeks to effectively erase the distinction between self and other, by loving the other as one's self.

In *Siegfried*, *agape* seems to have triumphed over *thumos*. But in *Götterdämmerung* the tables are turned, and *thumos*—the human desire for power and prestige—proves ineradicable. Love does not win in the

---

[5] Though there is undeniably an erotic dimension to Wagner's championing of "love," the "love" that he most often seems to have in mind corresponds most closely to *agape*, not *eros*.

end, as Wagner originally intended. And neither does *thumos*—for the simple reason that Brünnhilde puts the torch to Siegfried's funeral pyre and sets in motion a blaze that consumes the entire world. Hagen is dragged down by the Rhine daughters, still screaming for the ring. In the end, everything is consumed—including the good (love) and the bad (power lust and greed). So, the next question we must ask—our final, major question—is this: what is it that "wins" at the end of the *Ring*? What do Brünnhilde and her act of destruction at the finale of *Götterdämmerung* represent?

# Chapter Nine:
# *Gelassenheit*

We can say that the plot of the *Ring* is simply this: Western man, in the person of Wotan, finally awakens to the destructiveness of his *thumotic* nature and wills his own end.[1] This comes initially in the form of *agape*, the negation of *thumos*. Wotan allows himself and the rule of *thumos* to be displaced by the hopeful, new world ruled by *agape*. But, alas, it is not to be. *Thumos*, in its degenerate forms, re-emerges and destroys the love of Siegfried and Brünnhilde.

Now, one could claim, however, that love *does* win in the end. When Brünnhilde sets the torch to the funeral pyre and consumes the entire imperfect world, with all its lust for power, she does so out of love for Siegfried. This is partly true, but something more is at work here. To see this, we must look closely at what Brünnhilde says at the climax of the drama. As the fire blazes she speaks of Siegfried to her horse, Grane: "Does the laughing fire lure you to him? — Feel how the flames burn in my breast, effulgent fires seize hold of my heart: to clasp him to me while held in my arms and in mightiest love and to be wedded to him!"[2] But earlier she says something far more significant, calling to Wotan: "[It] was I whom the purest man had to betray, that a woman might grow wise. — Do I now know what you need? All things, all things, all things I know [*Alles! Alles! Alles weiss ich*], all is clear to me now!"

---

[1] See my review of Duchesne's *Uniqueness of Western Civilization* for a discussion of how Western man is preeminently *thumotic* man.

[2] Spencer, 350.

What is this wisdom that Brünnhilde has acquired, this knowledge of all things? (Note how Wagner emphasizes *four times* that she now knows *all*.) Wagner actually wrote two other versions of Brünnhilde's final speech. The earliest version (from 1852) is referred to by scholars as the "Feuerbach ending," because it so clearly conveys Feuerbach's influence on Wagner's original idea for the meaning of the *Ring*, prior to his reconceiving it. In this ending, Brünnhilde says that she leaves behind her "a world without rulers." (In the final version, of course, she destroys the world!) And she says that she bequeaths to the world not wealth, not gold, not splendor, not "smooth-tongued custom's stern decree" but instead "love" alone.[3]

Much more interesting is the so-called "Schopenhauer ending" of 1856, which I will quote at length:

> I depart from the world of desire,
> I flee forever the home of delusion;
> the open gates
> of eternal becoming
> I close behind me now:
> to the holiest chosen land,
> free from desire and delusion,
> the goal of the world's migration,
> redeemed from reincarnation,
> the enlightened woman now goes.
> The blessed end
> of all things eternal,
> do you know how I attained it?
> Grieving love's
> profoundest suffering
> opened my eyes for me:
> I saw the world end.

---

[3] Spencer, 362–63.

Ultimately, Wagner rejected this too—but for different reasons, I believe. While Wagner clearly did change his mind about the "Feuerbach ending," and came to feel that it was not what he wanted to convey, I do not think this is the case with the "Schopenhauer ending." In fact, it expresses almost exactly what he had come to believe was the "message" of the *Ring*. Perhaps he rejected it because it was too explicitly philosophical—too Buddhist, really. And so he went with the somewhat more ambiguous speech now familiar to us. In both cases—that of the Schopenhauer ending, and the one that Wagner finally decided on—the underlying ideas are the same. The wisdom Brünnhilde has gained—her knowledge of all things—is the realization that this world really is a veil of *maya*, and that the only appropriate standpoint is that of renunciation.

I have already discussed how there is a theory of history—of "ages"—within the *Ring*. The shift from Wagner's early, anarchist conception to his later "Schopenhauerian" conception is marked by a shift in his understanding of time. In true socialist fashion, the earlier Wagner saw time, or history, as linear and progressing towards a new world without masters, ruled only by love. The Wagner of the mature *Ring*, however, sees time as cyclical. At the end of *Götterdämmerung*, as the entire world is consumed by fire and flood, we hear the familiar strains of the "Rhine music" from the beginning of *Das Rheingold*. What this suggests, as many have pointed out, is that the end returns to the beginning: after the cataclysm, the world will be renewed; things will happen all over again in an "eternal recurrence of the same." (The *Ring* is a ring, in other words.) A cyclical view of time, of endlessly repeating cycles of ages, is suggested here.

Wagner's "Schopenhauerian" standpoint sounds awfully grim. But just listen to the "Rhine music" that closes *Götterdämmerung*—again, reminding us of the beginning of *Das Rheingold*. It is bright and hopeful. "Renunciation" need not be an angry rejection of the world. It need not require us to become monks—and it certainly does not require us to kill ourselves (in a famous essay, Schopenhauer opposed suicide). What it involves is recognizing that the world, or life, is suffering. And suffering, as the Buddha taught, is caused by desire. We think that the satisfaction of certain desires will make us happy, but in fact we only become ensnared in desiring more. There is therefore no *true* satisfaction in the satisfaction of desire—this is just a trap.

The first step toward true satisfaction, for the Schopenhauerian-Buddhist perspective, consists in recognizing this. The next step is not to eliminate our desires, for that is impossible, but to *change our relationship to our desires*. We learn not to identify with our desires and to become largely indifferent to whether they are satisfied. But this perspective is impossible without coming to see the world for what it is: as a never-ending cycle of suffering: suffering, followed by momentary satisfaction, followed by suffering again. This is what Brünnhilde comes to see. This is why she repeatedly tells us that she now knows *alles*. And she brings the world to an end—symbolically conveying a state of complete and total detachment from the travails of life. But again, the tone at the end of the *Ring* is bright and filled with promise. The lesson we are meant to take away is that we must indeed detach ourselves from the world—that we must die to it, in a sense—but that we may live in the world at the same time, in a transformed and enlightened state. Wagner wrote to a correspondent that the *Ring* "teaches us that we must learn to die"[4] Joseph Campbell liked to call this standpoint "joyful participation in the sorrows of the world."[5] And this is clearly the approach to life that Wagner himself came to adopt.

Wagner's incorporation of this (optimistic) Schopenhauerian standpoint into the *Ring* is, of course, another chapter in the story of his engagement with the Germanic tradition. Though I have referred to Buddhism in explaining these ideas, Schopenhauer claimed that he arrived at all of his basic theories prior to his encounter with Eastern thought. And, indeed, there is a tradition of what we might call "Germanic Buddhism," going back to the medieval German mystics.

Meister Eckhart and the anonymous author of the fourteenth-century *Theologia Germanica* both refer to a concept called *Gelassenheit*. This is a noun formed from the past participle of the verb *lassen*, which means "to leave, allow, or let." It could thus be translated literally as "leaving" or "allowing" (or, more awkwardly "leavingness" or "allowingness," since the German suffix -*heit* is usually equivalent to English -ness). The term shows up in Heidegger's work as well, and has been translated into English (very imperfectly) as "letting beings be." *Gelassenheit* is essentially the same attitude of detachment or renunciation taught by the Buddha and by Schopenhauer: living in the world, while remaining unaffected by it—letting things be, without identifying with them.

Of course, as Julius Evola taught us, there is anoth-

---

[4] Quoted in Lee, 94.
[5] See, for example, Joseph Campbell, *Myths of Light: Eastern Metaphors of the Eternal*, ed. David Kudler (Novato, California: New World Library, 2003), 126.

er dimension to this standpoint, which gets lost when it is misrepresented as being about peace and love and nonviolence.[6] Indeed, the path of "joyful participation in the sorrows of the world" is the path of the warrior. And it is only possible through a kind of *internalization of thumos*. To follow this path one must master one's desires, or one's attachment to desire. Instead of an enemy "out there" that I seek to subdue, the enemy is internal: it is my attachment to ephemera, my bad habits, my restless mind that gives me no peace. I must conquer these things. Only then can I be free. One can thus see that the standpoint of Brünnhilde at the climax of the *Ring* is actually a further transformation, or "sublimation," of *thumos*. She is only able to light the pyre because she has broken her attachment to the world—the supreme act of self-mastery, the supremely free act.

As Gustav Meyrink writes (in passages excerpted in Julius Evola's *Introduction to Magic*), "There is no god above an awakened man."[7] At the end of the *Ring* we thus really do leave behind gods—by becoming godlike ourselves. Of course, in the warrior the achievement of *Gelassenheit* allows him to continue to fight, conquer, and kill—now with complete detachment, free of concern for the outcome. It allows him to say "yes" to strife and conflict and to the brutality of life. This is the standpoint that is taught to Arjuna in the *Bhagavad-Gita*—the standpoint Evola has referred

---

[6] See Julius Evola, *The Doctrine of Awakening: The Attainment of Self-Mastery According to the Earliest Buddhist Texts*, trans. H. E. Musson (Rochester, Vermont: Inner Traditions, 1996).

[7] Paraphrasing Meyrink, in Julius Evola and the UR Group, *Introduction to Magic*, trans. Guido Stucco (Rochester, VT: Inner Traditions, 2001), 40.

to as the "Traditional Doctrine of Battle and Victory."[8]

And we find this same warrior spirit in the North, in the Germanic tradition, expressed vividly in the Eddas and Sagas—in all the sources that took possession of Wagner when he planned and composed the *Ring*. One wishes that Wagner had explicitly realized that Brünnhilde's "path of renunciation" is also the path of the warrior, but it seems he did not. (Too bad Evola wasn't around to advise him that the Buddha was a *Kshatriya*.)

And yet what we must conclude is that in the message of the *Ring* there is in fact no fundamental departure from the spirit of the pagan, Germanic tradition. Here we come full circle, back to the original intention of this little book, which was not just to place Wagner within the Germanic tradition (broadly construed), but to defend the *Ring* as a grand synthesis—and elaboration—of the Germanic mythological material.

One wishes, again, that Wagner's attitude toward *thumos*—in its higher forms—had been affirmative. And that he could have said "yes" to our Faustian (or Odinic) Western nature and celebrated our desire for knowledge and mastery. It would be left to Wagner's erstwhile friend Friedrich Nietzsche to do all of that. And clearly Nietzsche's own affirmation of "will to power" was born of the same frustration with the *Ring* that we feel. It says so much, including much that is right, but ultimately we cannot make it say exactly what we really want it to.

This need not trouble us, however, for the imperfections of the *Ring* pale in comparison to its sublime virtues. At the very least, Wagner can certainly be said

---

[8] See Julius Evola, "The Traditional Doctrine of Battle and Victory," in *Tyr*, vol. 2 (Atlanta: Ultra, 2004).

to have succeeded in creating a modern equivalent of Greek tragedy. But it is crucial to note that it was Germanic myth, not Greek myth, that gave birth to this "total work of art" — which stands, in this author's estimation at least, as the greatest artistic achievement of the modern era.

# Appendix: Suggestions for Exploring Wagner

The best way to approach Wagner for the first time is to listen—repeatedly—to just about any of the many CD compilations of "musical highlights" from his operas. There are innumerable discs that offer a "compact *Ring*" or a "*Ring* without words," and just about all of them are worth listening to. Then, when one has developed an affinity for Wagner's music, one should attempt to either see live performances of his operas, or watch video recordings. Probably the best opera to begin with is, in fact, the *Ring*'s first part: *Das Rheingold*. As Joscelyn Godwin has pointed out to me, it is the only opera ever written that has no human characters.

As for video recordings of the *Ring*, the best available is from 1980: the controversial Patrice Chéreau production staged at Bayreuth. Also worth a look is the Metropolitan Opera's production, staged by Otto Schenk. Though the Schenk production is far more "traditional," the Chéreau production is superior in many ways—especially in its pacing. The Met's recent, ghastly Robert Lepage production (featuring the notorious "Wagner machine"[1]) looks better on video (thanks to all the closeups) than it did live, and features excellent performances. All of these productions

---

[1] See Jef Costello, "Rage Against the Machine: A Very American *Ring* Cycle," in *The Importance of James Bond & Other Essays,* ed. Greg Johnson (San Francisco: Counter-Currents, 2017).

are available for purchase as DVDs or Blu-rays.

As for reading material, one could start with the libretti of the *Ring*. The best translation is by Stewart Spencer in *Wagner's Ring of the Nibelung: A Companion*. The best books *about* Wagner are Deryck Cooke's *I Saw the World End: A Study of Wagner's Ring* (of which I have made extensive use), Bryan Magee's *The Tristan Chord: Wagner and Philosophy*, and Magee's *Aspects of Wagner* (probably the book to begin with: it is quite short and offers a good overview of Wagner's work and its meaning).

# INDEX

**A**
*Addresses to the German Nation* (Fichte), 8
Aesir, 37
*agape*, 91–92, 93
Age of Gods, 30, 59, 61, 83
Age of Heroes, 59, 83–84
Age of Men, 60, 88; see also Kali Yuga, Wolf Age
Age of Titans, 59–61
Agnar, 41
Alberich, 23–25, 28–31, 37–39, 44–46, 49, 60, 66, 69, 70–74, 79, 90–91; see also Elberich
Andvara-falls, 44
Andvari, 37–38, 40, 44–46
Aristotle, 50
Arjuna, 98
*Art and Climate* (Wagner), 57
*Art and Revolution* (Wagner), 8–9
*Artwork of the Future, The* (Wagner), 10, 62, 69, 71
*arya*, 72
ash tree (in *Die Walküre* Act I), 1, 26, 43
*Aspects of Wagner* (Magee), 8n2, 102

Attila the Hun, 13; see also King Etzel

**B**
Bach, J. S., 1
Bakunin, Mikhail, 10, 49
Bayreuth, 101
*Bhagavad-Gita*, 98
*Brot af Sigurdarkvida*, 45n9
Brünnhilde, 1, 13, 18, 26–28, 30–33, 36, 38–39, 41, 43, 47, 49, 51, 64, 66–67, 69, 74–75, 77–79, 82, 84, 88, 90, 92–96, 98–99; relationship with Wotan, 27, 65, 67, 74–75, 77–79
Buddha, 96–97, 99
Buddhism, 95–97
Burgundians, 31, 35, 45n12

**C**
Campbell, Joseph, 97
Chéreau, Patrice, 101
China, 56
Cleary, Collin, 55n8, 56n9, 70n2
cloak of invisibility, 44, 47
Cooke, Deryck, 3n3, 10n4, 13n5, 17, 19–21, 39, 44–45, 57, 61–62,

64–65, 67–70, 73–74, 77, 78n5, 82, 85, 102
cosmopolitanism, 8, 10
Costello, Jef, 101n1
curses, 24, 29, 37, 84

**D**

Dark Elves, 37, 46; see also Dwarfs
*Das Rheingold*, see *Rheingold, Das*
death of Siegfried, 11, 33, 35–36, 90
*Decline of the West, The* (Spengler), 55n8
desire, 96–98
*Deutsche Heldensage, Die* (Grimm), 15
*Deutsche Mythologie* (Grimm), 15, 52
*Dies Irae*, 54
*Die Walküre*, see *Walküre, Die*
*Discourse on the Origin of Inequality, The* (Rousseau), 89n2
*Doctrine of Awakening: The Attainment of Self-Mastery According to the Earliest Buddhist Texts* (Evola), 98n6
Dorn, Heinrich, 7
dragons, 1, 29, 32, 36, 37, 84
Duchesne, Ricardo, 55n8, 90n4, 93n1
Dwarfs (race), 23–24, 37, 39, 44, 45n12, 46, 66; see also Dark Elves

**E**

*Eddas*, 4, 35, 40, 62, 99; see also *Poetic Edda*; *Prose Edda*
Elberich, 45–46; see also Alberich
envy, 69–74, 88, 91
Erda, 17, 24–25, 30, 39, 59, 61, 65, 74, 77; see also Wala and Urwala
*eros*, 91n5
*Essence of Christianity, The* (Feuerbach), 85n10
eternal recurrence of the same, 95
Etzel, 13; see also Atilla the Hun
Evola, Julius, 97–99

**F**

Fafner, 24–25, 28–29, 37–38, 74, 84; see also giants
fascism, 86
Fasolt, 24, 39, 47; see also giants
Faust, 64
*Faust* (Goethe), 64, 67
*Faust Overture* (Wagner), 64
Faustian Soul (of Western Man), 54–59, 84, 99
fear, 29, 30
Feuerbach, Ludwig, 4, 9,

49, 85, 94–95
Fichte, J. G., 8, 63
*Fliegende Holländer, Der*, 5
Flying Dutchman, 6, 64
free man, 9, 77, 79
free will, 76, 81
Freia, 16, 23–24, 37–38, 63, 74; compared to Idun, 38
Fricka, 16, 26, 40, 59, 65, 73, 76, 79, 91
Frigg, 39
Frodo, 3

## G

*Gelassenheit*, 93–100
*Germania*, 17
German nationalism, 7–8, 10, 86
Giants, 23–24, 28, 59, 63
Gibichungs, 10, 31
Giuki, 41, 47
Giuki, sons of, 41
Gnita Heath, 37
Godwin, Jocelyn, 101
Goethe, 64
golden apples, 24, 38
*Götterdämmerung*, 11, 30, 35, 39, 42, 47, 51, 59–61, 67, 96; synopsis, 30–34; analysis, 88–92
Gram, 41
Grane, 27, 34, 93
great chain of being, 50
greed, 49, 51, 71–72, 84–85, 88, 90–92
Greek tragic drama, 5, 8, 59, 100
Grimhild, 47
Grimm, Jacob and Wilhelm, 15–17, 39, 52, 53
*Grimnismal*, 39
Gunther, 31–33, 36, 47, 60, 88–91; compared to Wotan, 90–91
Gutrune, 31–33, 36, 43, 88–91; compared to Wotan, 90–91

## H

Hagen, 31–34, 36, 41, 46, 60, 88–92
Hatto, A. T., 3
Hegel, G. W. F., 4, 5, 49–50, 86
Heidegger, Martin, 97
*Heldenbuch*, 14, 45
Hellas, 58
Hercules, 58
Hesperides, garden of, 38
Hjordis, 40, 41, 43
Hlidskjalf, 55
Hogni, 36, 46
honor, 33, 71–72, 76, 90–91
Hreithmar, 37
Huginn and Muninn, 55
Hunding, 25–27, 40

## I

*I Saw the World End: A Study of Wagner's Ring* (Cooke), 3n3, 102
Idun's apples, 37–38;

compared to Freia, 38
*Importance of James Bond & Other Essays, The* (Costello), 101n1
India, 56, 58
*Introduction to Magic* (Evola), 98

**J**
Jesus, 3
Johnson, Greg, 50n2, 101n1

**K**
Kali Yuga, 60, 88; see also Age of Men, Wolf Age
Kriemhild, 36

**L**
Lang, Fritz, 47, 86
*Lay of Sigrdrifa*; see *Sigrdrifumal*
Lee, M. Owen, 51n4, 53-54, 56, 60
*Leitmotive*, 61-62
LePage, Robert, 101
*Lied vom hürnen Seyfrid, Das*, 35, 44, 46
Liszt, Franz, 51, 60
Loge, 16, 23-25, 28, 31, 40, 64-67, 69, 72, 79; as intellect, 64-67, 79; as *technē*, 66; relationship with Wotan, 64, 67, 69
Logi, 16
*logos*, 65
*Lohengrin*, 5-6

*Lokasenna*, 40
Loki, 16, 37, 40, 44
*Lord of the Rings, The* (Tolkien), 2-3, 28n1
love, 70, 78, 85, 91n5-95, 98; Alberich renounces, 23, 69-70, 72, 74; and Hagen, 90; as "fellow-feeling," 85-86; of Brünnhilde and Siegfried, 1, 30-33, 78, 82, 84, 88, 93; of Brünnhilde and Wotan, 74, 77-78; of Gutrune and Siegfried, 89; of Siegmund and Sieglinde, 26, 78, 95; of Wotan and Siegfried, 27, 77; renunciation of, 44, 70; versus *eros*, 91n5; Wagner's concept of, 85-87; Wotan's ability to love, 62-63, 65, 74-75, 77, 80
Ludwig II, 11

**M**
Magee, Bryan, 8n2, 9n3, 62, 102
Magee, Elizabeth, 35-36
Marx, Karl, 49
master-slave dialectic, 49-50
*Maya*, 95
Meister Eckhart, 97
*Meistersinger von Nürn-*

*berg, Die*, 6
Mephistopheles, 64–65
*Metropolis* (film by Lang), 86
Metropolitan Opera, 101
Meyrink, Gustav, 98
Middle High German, 7, 12, 46
Mime, 28–30, 32, 36, 38, 39, 72, 91
Mimir, 36, 56, 61–62
Mozart, 1, 2n1
myths, 1, 3–5, 13, 19–22, 54, 57, 63; Germanic, 1–5, 7, 11–12, 19, 54, 100; Greek, 60, 100; Northern European, 2, 21, 57; Scandinavian, 9, 11–12, 15, 16

# N
narcissism, 90
National Socialism, 2n2, 86
nature, man's alienation from, 57–63, 73, 69–70, 73, 82–85
Nazism, see National Socialism
*Nebelkap*, 46; see also Tarnhelm
Nerthus, 17, 39
Nibelheim, 24, 46, 72
Nibelungen (race), 13, 45n12–46
*Nibelungen, Die* (film), 47
*Nibelungen* (opera by Dorn), 7
*Nibelungenlied*, 3–4, 7, 9–13, 19–21, 35–36, 44–47, 82
"Nibelungen-Myth as Sketch for a Drama, The," 39n7
Nibelungs (race), 24, 35, 39, 44, 49
Nietzsche, Friedrich, 69, 73, 84, 99
Niflheim, 46
noble savage, 83
*Nornagests thattr*, 14, 20, 44
Norns, 30–31, 55, 59–61, 73
North, Richard, 38n3
*Nothung*, 26–30, 41, 43, 77; see also spear (Wotan's)

# O
Odin, 1, 37–39, 41–43, 55–56, 56n11, 63, 99; see also Wotan
Oedipus, 59
"Old Poem of Gudrun," 41
*Opera and Drama* (Wagner), 21
Otter, 37

# P
*Parsifal*, 5, 6
path of renunciation, 95–97, 99

path of the warrior, 98–99
*Perfect Wagnerite, The* (Shaw), 71n3
pessimism, 2, 50, 52
*Philosophy of Right* (Hegel), 86
*Pilgrimage to Beethoven and Other Essays* (Wagner, ed. Ellis), 39n7
Plato, 90
*Poetic Edda,* 13–14, 17–18, 20, 37–39, 41, 44, 47; see also *Eddas*
power, 24, 54, 59, 63–65, 67, 69–71, 73–75, 77, 80, 90, 92–93; of the Ring, 25, 27, 70; see also ring of power; will to power; Wotan, power of
power lust, 51, 73, 84–85, 88, 90, 92; see also power, will to power
prestige (unearned), 89–90, 92
*Prose Edda,* 13–14, 20, 35, 37–39, 44; see also *Eddas*
"Prose Sketch of the Ring" (Wagner), 10–11, 39, 49, 62, 63, 76, 81

**R**
Ragnarok, 38, 60
Regin, 36–39, 44
resentment, 69
*Rheingold, Das,* 11, 35, 40, 44, 47, 59–60, 64–66, 77, 95–96, 99, 101; synopsis, 23–25; analysis: 69–75
Rhine Daughters, 23, 32–34, 44, 59–60, 69, 73, 92
Rhine music, 34, 95–96
Rhinegold, 38, 44–45, 57, 60, 69
*Ring des Nibelungen, Der, passim*; "Feuerbach ending," 94–95; history in, 70–71; "love is the answer," 78; message of the *Ring,* 78, 95, 99; poetic form, 17–19; "Schopenhauer ending," 94–95; sources used by Wagner, 12–17, 19–22, 35–48; story of the *Ring,* 23–34, 93; Wagner's idea for the *Ring,* 10–11; world as *Maya,* 95; see also individual operas
ring of power, 24, 37, 38, 45, 90
Röckel, August, 53, 56
Rousseau, Jean-Jacques, 83, 89
runes, 47, 56, 63
rune-spell, 47

## S

sacrifice (Wotan's eye), 1, 56, 62
sagas, 3, 4, 15, 99; see also specific titles
Schelling, F. W. J., 50
Schenk, Otto, 101
Schopenhauer, Arthur, 2, 4, 22, 50–52, 54, 67, 94–97
self-awareness, 65, 67, 81–83
self-consciousness, 57, 82
Shaw, George Bernard, 71
Siegfried, 1, 7, 12–14, 18, 20, 27–33, 35–36, 38–41, 43–45, 47, 49, 56, 59–60, 67, 73–74, 76–78, 79–82, 84, 88–90, 93; slaying the dragon, 1, 37, 84n8
*Siegfried*; 11, 22, 91–92; synopsis, 28–30; analysis, 79–87
*Siegfrieds Tod*, 10, 49
Sieglinde, 25–28, 41, 43–44, 73, 76–78, 91
Siegmund, 1, 25–28, 31, 40–43, 63, 73, 76–78, 91
Signy, 40, 41, 42, 43
*Sigrdrifumal*, 18, 38n4, 47
Sigurd, 13, 37, 41, 43
Sinfjotli, 40, 42, 43
Smeagol, 28n1
Spear (Wotan's), 17, 25, 27, 30–31, 47, 59
Spencer, Stewart, 80, 102
Spengler, Oswald, 54–55, 55n8
*Stabreim*, 17, 19
Sturluson, Snorri, 5, 38n2
suffering, 94, 96
*Summoning the Gods* (Cleary), 70n2
sword in tree, 1, 26

## T

Tacitus, 17, 39
*Tannhäuser*, 5, 64
Tannhäuser, 64
Tarnhelm, 24, 28, 30, 32, 46–47; see also *Nebelkap*
*technē*, 66
*Theologia Germanica*, 97
*Thidreks saga*, 13–14, 45–46
Thorsson, Edred, 56n11
*thumos/thumotic*, 72, 90–92, 93
*Thus Spoke Zarathustra* (Nietzsche), 84n7
time, cyclical, 95
Tolkien, J. R. R., 2, 35
"Traditional Doctrine of Battle and Victory," (Evola), 99n2
*Tristan Chord: Wagner and Philosophy, The* (Magee) 9n3, 63n20, 102
*Tristan und Isolde*, 6, 11

tropics, 57–58

**U**
*Uniqueness of Western Civilization, The* (Duchesne), 55n8, 90n4, 93n1
universalism, 56

**V**
Valhalla, 1, 23–25, 27, 31–34, 37–38, 49, 67, 75, 78
Valkyries, 25–27, 30, 32, 36, 38, 88
*Volsunga saga*, 3, 13–14, 20–21, 35–44, 47, 82
*Völuspá*, 35, 39, 54
Völva, 39
Von Bern, Dietrich, 13
Von Harbou, Thea, 86n13

**W**
Wagner, Cosima, 82
Wagner, Richard, *passim*; anarchism, 10, 49, 53, 71, 84–85, 95; basic idea for the *Ring*, 10–11; concept of love ("fellow-feeling"), 85–7; conversion from revolutionary to pessimist, 51–52; Germanic identity, 53–54; nationalism, 7–10, 86–87; poetry, 3–5, 17–19; Radical Traditionalism, 49–50; Schopenhauer's influence on the *Ring*, 50–52; sources of the *Ring*, 12–17, 19–22, 35–48 time, understanding of, 95
*Wagner's Ring of the Nibelung: A Companion* (Spencer & Millington), 18n9, 102
*Wagner's Ring: Turning the Sky Around* (Lee), 51n4
Wala and Urwala, 39; see also Erda
*Walküre, Die*, 11, 25, 28, 35, 40, 51, 59, 66–67, 70, 74, 79; synopsis, 42–43; analysis, 76–78
Wälse, 25–26, 42, 43
Wälsungs, 42, 76
Waltraute, 32, 75
Wanderer (Wotan's disguise), 17, 26, 29, 35, 43, 55
wealth, 69–73, 84, 86, 88, 94
*What Is a Rune?* (Cleary), 55n8, 56n9
*Wieland der Schmied*, 6
Will (in Cleary), 70n2
Will (in Schopenhauer), 50
will to power, 59, 73, 99
wisdom, 31, 56, 61, 94–95
*Wôdan*, 15

Wolf Age, 60; see also Age of Men, Kali Yuga
Wolfe (alias of Wotan), 42, 76
*World as Will and Representation, The* (Schopenhauer), 50–51
world ash tree, see Yggdrasil
Wotan, 1, 15–16, 23–33, 39–40, 42–43, 47, 69–70, 72–75, 76–78, 79–84, 90–91, 93; and the West's Faustian soul, 49–68, 72, 83, 93; compared to Alberich, 31, 60, 72-4, 79, 90–91; compared to Gunther and Gutrune, 90–91; compared to Siegfried, 56, 79–82; consequences of missing eye, 80–82; his great sin, 83; his power, 25, 30, 31, 55, 63, 74; his self-awareness or self-understanding, 65, 67, 77, 81–83; his will, 67, 79; other characters as personifications of aspects of, 65, 79, 90–91; relationship with Loge, 64, 67, 69; with Brünnhilde, 27, 65, 67, 74–75, 77–79; see also Odin
Wuotan, 15–17

**Y**

Yggdrasil, 31, 61-63, 73, 75, 82
Ymir, 39, 63

# ABOUT THE AUTHOR

COLLIN CLEARY, Ph.D. is an independent scholar living in Sandpoint, Idaho. He is the author of *Summoning the Gods: Essays on Paganism in a God-Forsaken World* (2011) and *What Is a Rune?* (2015). He is one of the founders of *TYR: Myth-Culture-Tradition*, the first volume of which he co-edited. A Master in the Rune-Gild, his work has been translated into Czech, Danish, French, Portuguese, Russian, and Swedish.

www.ingramcontent.com/pod-product-compliance
Lightning Source LLC
LaVergne TN
LVHW041547070426
835507LV00011B/961